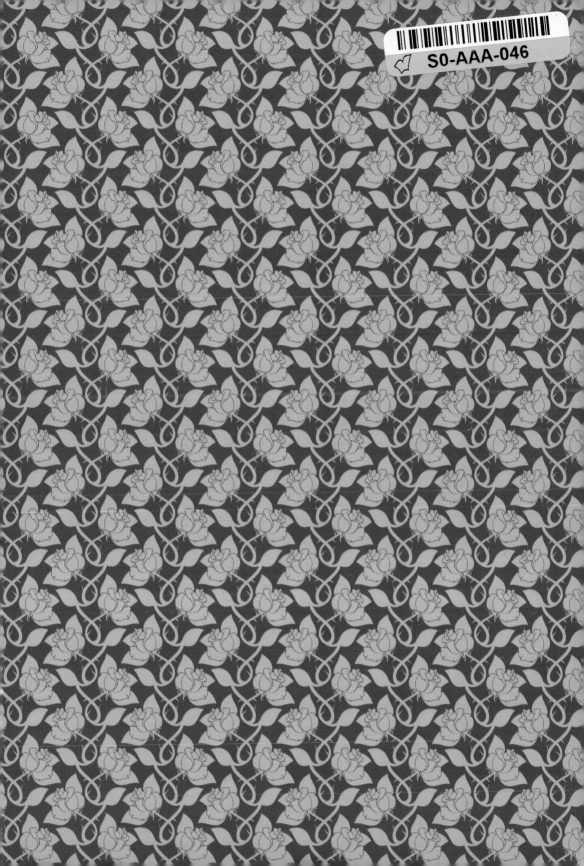

YELLOW ROSE
Recipes

YELLOW ROSE
Recipes

Over 120 Quick and Delicious
Vegan Creations with Kick

JOANNA VAUGHT

[handwritten inscription] Tasha,
you're super swell & you
know it!
Joanna

2007
Herbivore Magazine
1211 SE Stark
Portland, OR 97214

Printed in Canada
First edition

ISBN 978-0-9801440-0-0

Cover photos by Shayne Berry
Cover design by Josh Hooten
Interior design by Josh Hooten and Tom Filepp
Illustrations by Amanda Chronister

Contact the author through www.yellowroserecipes.com
Wholesale, press, and otherwise contact editor@herbivoremagazine.com

Forward
by Isa Chandra Moskowitz

Someone somewhere supposedly once said that a home cook will make only 2 recipes out of every cookbook on their shelf. Enter *Yellow Rose Recipes*.

What I love about Joanna's recipes is that they are lived in. It's not that she has traveled to a tiny but progressive village in France and brought back some homespun yet mystical culinary secret. It's that she knows her away around the kitchen. It's that there *is* no big secret—just good food with simple ingredients prepared for maximum flavor. These are recipes you can trust.

In these pages you'll find an absence of lofty current food trends. No "on a bed of this" or "with a kiss of" that. There is no need for the whimsical and pretentious, recipes that look good on paper but waste your time and money. Not when you've got Jalapeno Corncakes, Lemon Artichoke Pesto, Mustard Crusted Seitan and Kasha Varnishkes. Sure, she puts cumin in this Jewish staple, but she's from Texas and this is her world. In fact, her Texas upbringing informs a lot of Joanna's food as well as her take on what makes a perfect meal: Strong flavors, don't-be-shy portions, and good friends to share it all with—not to mention a smart dose of efficiency and economy.

There are a lot of fancy cookbooks out there that are more fun to look at, or show off to guests, than to cook from. *Yellow Rose Recipes*, while fun to look at, will be one of those covered-in-food-dog-eared-pages editions to your collection. So curl up with a nice chunk of Aloha Bread and dip your toes into some good vegan eats.

From Brooklyn, Isa Chandra Moskowitz

Dedications & Thanks

This book is for Matthew, who made it possible for to me to write in my spare time while working full time (and pregnant!) without losing my mind; who was my first and most honest recipe tester; and who did a lot of dishes and ate a lot of leftovers over the course of my writing this book. Thanks, Mokin.

And for Milo Bear, who is already inspiring me to be a better and healthier person.

Thanks to my family. Thanks especially to my parents, who have always supported my dietary choices and gone out of their way to accommodate me.

Thanks to my friends. Thanks especially to Melissa, who I love like sheep.

Thanks to my Portland vegan pals, with whom I blissfully geek out about food on a regular basis. Thanks especially to Josh and Michelle, who trusted me to be their first cookbook.

Thanks to Amanda Chronister, who did the amazing illustrations for the book. I wish I were as cute in real life as I am when you draw me, Amanda.

Finally, a huge thanks to all of my recipe testers: Michelle Anderson, Emily Berna, Chaya Branley, Jenna Brooks, Kim Carpenter, Amanda Chronister, Michelle Citrin, Raelene Coburn, Maeve Connor, Allicia Cormier, Lisa Coulson, Jessica DeNoto, Amanda Dickie, Kate Flagg, Michelle Graves, Ashley Griffeth, Rose Hermalin, Anna Hood, Katie Hubbard, Connie Leonard, Katie Marggraf, Joni Newman, Jen Oaks, Rebecca Padrick, Staci Rudnitsky, Amanda Sacco, Dwan Tape, Michele Thompson-Brayton, Veronica Timan, Carly Wellman, Shanell Dawn Williams.

Table of Contents

Introduction

Let's start with the obvious: I love food. I love eating; I love restaurants, potlucks, and dinner parties; I love looking at pictures of other people's food on the internet. I can spend twenty minutes talking with another food lover about the best place in town to buy greens. I watch even the pathetically bad cooking shows on TV, because even bad food is entertaining. I collect cookbooks the way that some people collect shoes or matchbooks. One night not so long ago, my partner and I had been in bed, both awake but not talking, and I asked him what he was thinking about. He said: "Gentrification. What are you thinking about?" "Perfecting a vegan hollandaise sauce."

The only thing that I love more than food is cooking. My idea of the perfect Saturday is to: wake up and make a little breakfast; flip through some of my favorite recipes and works-in-progress and compile a shopping list while drinking my coffee; go to the farmers market and the grocery store; come home and spend the rest of the afternoon cooking while listening to music or NPR.

My hope is that if you bought this book, you love food, too. The good news is: if you don't love cooking yet, or are new to it, there is nothing so daunting, time-consuming, or overwhelming in this book that you will want to throw in the towel and throw my book across the room out of frustration.

My favorite world cuisines (Southern American, Mexican, Indian, Middle Eastern) all have the following in common: they use seasonal, local, and fresh produce, grains, and spices to create simple, delicious, quick-to-prepare meals—and they don't break the bank in the process. Preparing dishes from these cuisines has hugely influenced my own cooking over the last ten years. I don't make any recipe if I can tell from glancing at it that I'm going to spend more than $20 on the ingredients or more than 45 minutes on preparation alone.

I also loathe wasting food. In this cookbook, you'll see the same ten or twenty ingredients over and over again, and that's because I'm essentially a cheapskate who likes to get the most bang out of my buck. If I buy a bunch of parsley for tabouli, you can bet that I'll make marinara, herbed polenta, dressing, or tapenade before the week is out.

I'm also guessing that if you bought this cookbook, you are—if not a vegetarian yourself—at least interested in vegetarian cooking, and that you have your reasons

to help you out, and then bring you a casserole the next day for good measure. That's another thing: Texans do not fart around about food. They take pride in it; they organize social functions around it; they serve big heaping portions of it.

When I had been living away from Texas for a year, I decided that I wanted some way to commemorate my Texas roots, so I chose to get a giant yellow rose (the state flower of Texas) tattooed on the inside of my left arm. Obviously! And the Texan influence didn't end at my Southern charms. My home state also plays a large role in my cooking, most notably my portion sizes and my tendency to think every dish could be improved with the addition of avocados, jalapeños, cilantro, or black beans. When it came time to name this book, *Yellow Rose Recipes* was the first choice.

for that. I know that I have mine. Whatever brought you to vegetarian cooking, I am happy to have you here.

So, what's with the title of the book? If you've flipped to the back, you might have seen that I currently reside in Portland, Oregon, but I spent the first 26 years of my life in Texas. I grew up in Houston, I went to college outside of Dallas, and from there, I spent five very happy years in Austin. Texas, for all its flaws and good old boy politicians, treated me very well and is largely responsible for who I am now. Texans are exceptionally good-hearted and kind, will bend over backwards

Thank you so much for picking up my cookbook and inviting me into your kitchen.

Stock Your Kitchen

I'm not going to pretend I have every single one of the following items in my kitchen at all times, but when I need to buy a pantry or bulk item, I like to get twice what I need for the recipe I'm making, so I have the extra in stock. Keeping up this practice will ensure a well-stocked pantry in no time and it's so much easier to make a meal if you already have almost everything you need within reach. Every item here shows up in at least two of my recipes.

Pantry:

agave nectar (see Glossary, pg. 185)
baking powder
baking soda
brown rice
canned artichoke hearts
canned beans (black, black eyed peas, garbanzo, kidney, pinto)
canned tomatoes (diced, whole)
canned tomato sauce
cornmeal
cornstarch
dried beans (black, black eyed peas, lentils, pinto, white)
dried fruits (raisins, cranberries)
dried herbs (dill, oregano, rosemary, thyme)
extracts (vanilla, almond)
flax seeds (see Glossary, pg. 185)
flours (brown rice, chickpea, unbleached all purpose, whole wheat pastry)
grains (barley, quinoa, whole wheat couscous, wild rice)

liquid smoke
maple syrup
mirin (see Glossary, pg. 185)
nondairy chocolate chips
nonstick cooking sprays (canola, canola with flour for baking, olive oil)
nut butters (almond, peanut)
nutritional yeast (see Glossary, pg. 185)
oils (canola, grapeseed, olive, peanut, sesame, toasted sesame)
polenta meal (see Glossary, pg. 185)
rolled oats
salts (iodized, kosher, sea salt)
silken tofu, asceptically packaged (see Glossary, pg. 185)
soy sauce
spices, spice mixes, dried sundries (black peppercorns, brown mustard seeds, cayenne, chili powder, cinnamon, cloves, crushed red pepper flakes, cumin, cumin seeds, curry powder, garlic powder, whole or ground nutmeg, onion powder, paprika, sage, turmeric, white peppercorns)
sugars (brown, turbinado, vegan granulated)
TVP (see Glossary, pg. 185)
tahini
tamari
tomato sauce
vinegars (balsamic, brown rice, cider, red wine, white wine)
vital wheat gluten (see Glossary, pg. 185)
whole grain pastas

Freezer:

frozen vegetables (corn, edamame, peas)
nuts, legumes, and seeds (almonds, cashews,
pecans, pistachios, pumpkin seeds, sesame
seeds, toasted sesame seeds, walnuts)
phyllo dough

A word about salt and pepper:

About half of these recipes were created and
tested using fine grain sea salt, and the other
half with good old girl-in-a-raincoat iodized
table salt. For this reason, and because people
have drastically different salt tolerances, I usually suggest in the body of the recipe salting
your recipes to taste or at the table, or I give
a range of added salt, such as 1/2-3/4 teaspoon. My suggestion, as you go through this
cookbook, is to start with just a little and add
as needed.

If you are a pregnant or nursing mother, it is
critical that you use iodized salt in your cooking. Iodine is sorely lacking in natural food
sources, aside from sea vegetables, which most
of us do not eat daily. A lack of dietary iodine
in the mother's diet can impair her child's
learning ability, neuromotor skills, and bone
development in utero and while nursing. Please
check your prenatal vitamins and multivita-
mins to ensure a 100% RDA of iodine, and
make a permanent switch to iodized salt. Keep
the sea salt around for occasional flavor or cre-
ating spice mixes.

Wherever pepper is mentioned, you'll see
"freshly ground black pepper." I strongly
recommend that you get a pepper grinder if
you don't already have one. Tinned ground
black pepper doesn't hold a candle to the taste
of freshly ground black pepper, and it's really
easy to overdo it with the pre-ground stuff.

One more thing about your kitchen:

I consider an oven thermometer to be as essential a piece of kitchen equipment as a good
knife, except that a good knife will run you
around $100 and oven thermometers start
at $5. There is a good chance that if you live
in an older house or apartment, your oven
is at least 15 degrees "off," which is enough
to completely ruin a recipe, especially baked
goods. When preheating an oven, make sure
that the thermometer has displayed the correct
temperature for at least five minutes before
putting your dish in there.

Breakfast

Tofu Scramble

If you're anything like me, you prepare your breakfast before you've even finished your coffee, through slitted eyes and with the lights off in the kitchen to delay the inevitable. I make it easier on myself by assembling a special scramble spice mix every week so I can throw the ingredients together in the morning without a whole lot of thought.

Ingredients

seasoning mix:

2 Tbs cumin

1 Tbs turmeric

1 Tbs garlic powder

1 Tbs onion powder

2 tsp salt

2 tsp paprika

1 tsp oregano

1 tsp thyme

1 tsp freshly ground black pepper

main recipe:

14-16 oz firm tofu, drained and gently pressed

2 tsp canola oil or non-hydrogenated margarine

1/2 cup onion, chopped

1 heaping Tbs tofu scramble seasoning mix

2 cloves garlic, minced

3 loosely packed cups of spinach, washed and torn

1/2 cup seeded (see Tips & Techniques, pg. 184) tomato, chopped

Instructions (serves 2-3)

COMBINE ALL SEASONING ingredients in an airtight container, close, and shake well to mix.

Cut your tofu into 3/4-1" cubes.

Heat oil in large skillet, preferably cast iron, to medium-high heat (or however high of heat you can keep it without reaching smoking point). Add onion and then tofu to skillet in single layer. Stir a little to coat tofu in oil and then sauté for 3-4 minutes. Keep heat as high as possible, but if tofu starts to burn, lower heat a little.

Add seasoning mix and garlic, stir well to coat, and sauté for 3-5 minutes. Use a wooden spoon or spatula to break apart and smoosh the cubes a little bit in the pan, so that the tofu isn't completely crumbled, but more scrambled looking.

Lower the heat to medium and add spinach to skillet without mixing it in—just let it sit on the top. Allow spinach to wilt a little, about 30 seconds, then mix it in. Add tomatoes and sauté for another minute or so before serving. Season at table with additional salt and pepper, if desired.

PESTO SCRAMBLE: Use half the amount of seasoning mix and add 2-3 Tbs prepared pesto sauce. Instead of chopping onions, slice into extremely thin half-rounds. Mix in 1 Tbs of vegan parmesan just before serving.

SAVORY MUSTARD SCRAMBLE: Add 1 tsp brown mustard seeds and 1 tsp Dijon mustard to the skillet with seasonings and garlic. Replace onion with shallots.

GREEK SCRAMBLE: Replace yellow onion with thinly sliced green onions. Replaced diced tomatoes with slivers of sun-dried tomatoes. Add sliced kalamata olives at same time as spinach.

MEXICAN SCRAMBLE: Use red onion instead of yellow onion. Add sliced mushrooms at same time as spinach and tomato. Add 1/8 tsp cayenne pepper. Garnish with chopped cilantro and sliced avocados, and salsa if so desired.

Perfect Oatmeal

Oatmeal with flax is the perfect breakfast for a chilly day, and I will fight anyone to the death who says otherwise. This is the way that I prepare it, and it's perfectly creamy without being too mushy.

Ingredients

Instructions (makes 1-2 servings)

1 cup rolled oats, not instant

1 1/3 cups water

pinch salt

1 Tbs flax seeds

2 Tbs soymilk

any of the following toppings:

raisins, dried cranberries, dried cherries

peach, apricot, or cherry compote

fresh berries

bananas

maple syrup

brown sugar

vanilla

walnuts

COMBINE OATS, water, and salt in a nonstick saucepan over high heat. As soon as oatmeal comes to a boil, reduce heat to a very low simmer and cook for 2-3 minutes or until water is completely absorbed, stirring regularly.

Stir in flax seeds and soymilk, remove from heat, and serve immediately with preferred toppings. My favorite combo is raisins, maple syrup, brown sugar, and vanilla.

Buckwheat Pancakes

Don't be thrown off by the fact that this batter resembles wet cement when mixed—
the taste is rich and warm.

Ingredients

1/2 cup buckwheat flour

1/2 cup whole wheat pastry flour

1/2 tsp baking powder

1/4 tsp baking soda

1/4 tsp salt

1 very ripe banana, mashed

2 Tbs maple syrup

pinch cinnamon

1 Tbs vinegar

1 cup + 2 Tbs soymilk

canola oil

extra banana slices

Instructions (makes 6-8 cakes)

IN A MEDIUM BOWL, mix flours, baking powder, baking soda, and salt.

In a large bowl, combine mashed banana, maple syrup, cinnamon, vinegar, and soymilk. Add flour mixture, stirring just enough to remove any lumps and make a pourable batter. If necessary, add a tablespoon more soymilk to thin out the batter.

Heat a thin layer of canola oil or spray in a large skillet or griddle over medium heat. Spoon pancake mixture directly onto the heated surface and cook until bubbles appear on surface. Flip carefully with a spatula and cook the second side until browned, about one minute. Serve immediately with extra banana slices and heated syrup.

Jalapeño Corn Cakes

Ingredients

Instructions (makes 6 medium or 8 small cakes)

1/2 cup cornmeal

1/2 cup whole wheat pastry flour

1/2 tsp baking powder

1/2 tsp salt

1/4 tsp baking soda

1/4 cup silken tofu

1 cup soymilk

2 Tbs non-hydrogenated margarine, melted

1 Tbs agave nectar

1/2 cup fresh or thawed frozen corn kernels

1 jalapeño, cut into thin rounds

canola oil

COMBINE CORNMEAL, flour, baking powder, salt, and baking soda in a large bowl.

In a medium bowl, use a fork to smoosh the tofu and break it up. Add soymilk and whisk briskly with the tofu until well-combined. Add margarine and agave nectar and mix well.

Add wet ingredients to the dry and mix until just combined. Add corn and jalapeño slices to the mix and use a wooden spoon to gently combine.

Heat a thin layer of canola oil or spray in a large skillet or griddle over medium heat. Spoon corn cake mixture directly onto the heated surface and cook until bubbles appear on surface. Flip carefully with a spatula and cook the second side until browned, about one minute. Serve immediately. Because of the margarine in the mixture, cakes can be served alone or with more margarine or maple syrup.

Buttermilk Biscuits

Soymilk mixed with a tablespoon of fresh lemon juice or vinegar replicates that slightly sour taste of buttermilk and gives these biscuits their distinct down home Southern flavor.

Ingredients

Instructions (makes 8-12 biscuits)

1 cup whole wheat pastry flour

1 cup unbleached all purpose flour

1 Tbs sugar

2 1/2 tsp baking powder

1/2 tsp salt

1/4 tsp baking soda

3/4 cup soymilk

1 Tbs fresh lemon juice or vinegar

3 Tbs canola oil

1 Tbs melted non-hydrogenated margarine

PREHEAT YOUR OVEN TO 450°. Sift together in a large bowl: flours, sugar, baking powder, baking soda, and salt.

In a small bowl or mixing cup, stir together soymilk and lemon juice. Whisk in oil.

Create a well in the flour mixture and pour in soymilk mixture. Mix together well. Dough should be pretty tacky to the touch but well-mixed.

On a lightly floured surface and with hands lightly floured, knead (see Glossary, pg. 185) dough gently for a minute or so. If dough is still too tacky, knead a little extra flour into the dough. Roll out dough to 1/2-3/4-inch thickness. A thicker dough will result in taller biscuits, if that's what you like.

Using a drinking glass, cut out biscuits and transfer to an ungreased cookie sheet, dipping glass in flour in between cuts. With the extra dough, roll out again and cut a few more biscuits out.

Bake for 12-15 minutes or until golden brown, then brush the tops with melted margarine as soon as they're out of the oven. Serve warm with Almond Milk Gravy (pg. 83).

Rosemary Home Fries

With a little prep the night before, it's easy to have home fries with your tofu scramble in the morning. You can sub dill for the rosemary in this recipe if you're a dill freak, or you can do half and half.

I sometimes opt not to remove the garlic and just eat them straight from the pan, but if you're serving other people, you might want to warn them so they don't unexpectedly sink their teeth into a whole clove of garlic thinking it's a little potato.

Ingredients

1 1/2 lbs small red potatoes, scrubbed and unpeeled

1 Tbs olive oil

4-6 cloves garlic, crushed

1 Tbs fresh rosemary, chopped

1 tsp kosher or sea salt

1/4 tsp freshly ground black pepper

Instructions (serves 4-6)

THE NIGHT BEFORE: In a large pot, cover potatoes with salted cold water, then boil until tender or easily pierced with a fork, about 20 minutes. Drain potatoes and let them cool in the colander, then transfer them back to the pot and put the pot in the fridge with plastic wrap on top to chill overnight. (If you want to do this on the morning of, drain and let the potatoes cool for 10 minutes or so before cutting them, so they're cool enough to handle.)

In the morning, take the potatoes out of the fridge and halve or quarter each potato into 3/4-1" chunks. Heat oil in a large heavy-bottomed skillet over medium-high heat. Add potatoes in a single layer and reduce to medium heat. If you can't fit them all in one pan, do this in batches, as it's critical that potatoes are in a single layer. Resisting the urge to move them around the pan, cook until golden brown, about 5-7 minutes. Add garlic to pan. Use tongs or spatula to turn the potatoes over in the pan and cook other side for another 5-7 minutes. Crumble the rosemary between your fingers into the pan and use spatula to toss potatoes again. Cover and cook for another 5-7 minutes.

Turn off the heat. Fish out garlic cloves, add salt and pepper, stir to coat the potatoes, and serve immediately.

Cherry Almond Granola

Packed! With! Protein! This granola saved me in the first trimester of my pregnancy when I needed 70g of protein per day, but had zero appetite and could only tolerate certain foods. A serving of this granola with half a cup of soymilk is 20g of protein.

Ingredients

3/4 cup packed brown sugar

1/2 cup vanilla soy protein powder or soymilk powder

1/2 cup agave nectar

1/2 cup white grape or apple juice

2 Tbs canola oil

2 tsp almond extract

5 cups rolled oats

1/2 cup amaranth

1/4 cup whole flax seeds

1 cup dried cherries

1 cup slivered almonds

Instructions (makes 8-12 servings)

PREHEAT OVEN TO 375°. Spray a 9x13" baking pan with nonstick cooking spray.

In a medium sauce pan over medium-low heat, combine sugar, protein powder, agave nectar, juice, oil, and almond extract. Whisk until sugar is dissolved. Set aside.

In a large bowl, combine oats, amaranth, flax seeds, cherries, and almonds and toss well to combine. Drizzle with sugar mixture and mix well. Pour in baking pan.

Bake for 20 minutes, remove and stir well, and bake for another 20-30 minutes or until golden brown. Wait until completely cool (15-20 minutes) before storing in an airtight container.

Zucchini Muffins

My boyfriend loves zucchini muffins. Specifically, he loves the zucchini muffins made by the bakery a few blocks from our house, and when we go on long walks, he tends to navigate us towards the store to get a muffin. The first time that I offered to make him the muffins, he said, "I don't know, are you going to make them too...healthy?" After multiple attempts, this is the least healthy-tasting and therefore most pleasing muffin to his tastebuds. Please, no one tell him that they're still good for him.

If you don't have a lemon, zest from any citrus fruit will do.

Ingredients

1 cup unbleached all purpose flour

1 cup whole wheat pastry flour

1 Tbs baking powder

1/2 tsp salt

1/4 tsp cinnamon

1/4 tsp nutmeg

1 cup shredded zucchini, packed (about one medium zucchini)

1/2 cup sugar

2 Tbs canola oil

1 tsp vanilla

1/4 cup plain soy yogurt

zest from one medium lemon

3/4 cup soymilk or vanilla hemp milk

1/3 cup raisins

1/4 cup chopped pecans (optional)

Instructions (makes 8 jumbo or 12 regular muffins)

PREHEAT OVEN TO 400°. Spray a muffin tin with non-stick cooking spray, preferably the kind with flour, or line with papers.

In a large bowl, sift together flours, baking powder, salt, cinnamon, and nutmeg. In a medium bowl, combine zucchini, sugar, canola oil, vanilla, soy yogurt, and soymilk. Add lemon zest to this mixture and mix in.

Make a well in the dry ingredients. Add zucchini mixture, raisins and pecans. Stir until just combined, making sure not to overmix. Don't worry if mixture seems too dry—it's fine. Fill each muffin well 2/3-3/4 full depending on desired size. Bake for 20 minutes or until a toothpick inserted in the center comes out clean.

Raisin Bran Muffins

These are based off my favorite muffin recipe from childhood called Six Week Muffins because the original recipe made 4 dozen muffins and the batter would keep for up to six weeks, covered, in the fridge.

In my house, as soon as my mom made them, she'd freeze half of them and transfer the rest to a gigantic Harvest Gold Tupperware container that lived on top of the fridge, and they are all my brothers and I ate, for every meal, and snacks in between. They never lasted more than a week.

Ingredients

3 cups raisin bran cereal

1 1/2 cups whole wheat pastry flour

1/2 cup whole flax seed

1 Tbs baking powder

1 tsp baking soda

1 1/2 cups vanilla soy or hemp milk

1 Tbs fresh lemon juice

1/2 cup sugar

1/2 tsp cinnamon

1/8 tsp ground cloves

3 Tbs canola oil

3 Tbs unsweetened applesauce

1 tsp vanilla

1/2 cup dried cranberries (optional)

Instructions (makes 16-20 muffins)

PREHEAT OVEN TO 375°. Spray muffin tins with nonstick cooking spray, preferably the kind with flour, or line with papers.

In a large bowl, mix raisin bran, flour, flax seed, baking powder, and baking soda. In a small bowl, add lemon juice to the soymilk and mix well. In a medium bowl, mix sugar, cinnamon, cloves, oil, applesauce, vanilla, and soymilk mixture. Add wet ingredients to dry ingredients and lightly mix, smooshing the bran flakes, until it's evenly mixed. Fold in cranberries if using them.

Distribute mixture evenly into muffin tins. Bake for 15-20 minutes or until toothpick comes out clean.

Photo: Michelle Citrin

Very Berry Muffins

Sometimes I get a little overzealous in the summer and cart home 6 pints of ripe
berries and am then faced with how two people are going to eat that many berries
before they go bad. This is my go-to muffin recipe and works well for strawberries,
raspberries, blueberries, and blackberries, or any combination of the above.

I use egg replacer powder in this recipe because I always have it and the whole point
of this recipe is to use what you have rather than run to the store. If you don't like it,
you can sub another egg replacer.

Ingredients

2 1/2 cups unbleached all purpose flour

1 Tbs egg replacer powder

2 tsp baking powder

1/2 tsp salt

1 1/2 cups soymilk

1/2 cup sugar

1/4 cup applesauce

2 Tbs canola oil

1 tsp vanilla

1 1/2 cups fresh berries

Instructions (makes 12 muffins)

PREHEAT OVEN TO 400°. Spray a muffin tin with nonstick
cooking spray, preferably the kind with flour, or line
with papers.

If using strawberries, slice each berry in four slices from
stem to tip, then in half.

In a large bowl, sift together the flour, egg replacer, baking
powder, and salt. In a small bowl, whisk together the soymilk, sugar, applesauce, oil, and vanilla. Add wet mixture
to dry and stir together well. Gently stir in berries.

Divide batter evenly in tin. Bake for 20 minutes or until
toothpick comes out clean.

Appetizers

Roasted Red Pepper Hummus

Ingredients

Instructions (makes 2 cups)

1 15 oz can chickpeas

4 oz bottled roasted red peppers, drained

2 garlic cloves

2 Tbs fresh lemon juice

1 Tbs tahini

1 tsp olive oil

1/2 tsp curry powder

1/2 tsp salt

1/4 tsp cumin

pinch freshly ground black pepper

DRAIN CHICKPEAS, reserving 1 tablespoon of liquid from the can. Add all ingredients, including reserved liquid, to the food processor and process until very smooth. Chill for at least two hours before serving.

Photo: Joni Newman

Roasted Eggplant and Garlic Hummus

Is this hummus? Is it baba ghanouj? Who knows. Who cares. It's the best of both worlds with hardly any fat and truckloads of flavor.

Ingredients

Instructions (makes 2 cups)

1 medium eggplant

8 cloves of garlic

1 can of chickpeas

1-3 Tbs of fresh lemon juice

1 tsp liquid from can of chickpeas

1 tsp olive oil

2 tsp tahini

1/4 cup parsley

1/2-1 tsp salt

1/8-1/4 tsp freshly ground black pepper

1/4 tsp ground cumin

PREHEAT YOUR OVEN TO 450°. Pierce eggplant with fork 4-6 times and wrap in foil. Wrap cloves of garlic (still in skin) in foil. Put both on a cookie sheet and bake them in the oven for 30-40 minutes.

Meanwhile, drain the chickpeas, reserving a little of the liquid and rinsing the chickpeas.

When eggplant and garlic are done roasting, remove foil and allow to cool for 10 minutes or until they can be handled with bare skin. Cut the eggplant in half and scoop out the insides into a food processor or blender. Peel the garlic cloves and add them. Add 1 Tbs of lemon juice (about 1/2 a medium lemon). Pulse or blend until smooth.

Add chickpeas, chickpea liquid, olive oil, tahini, parsley, 1/2 tsp of salt, tiny bit of black pepper, and cumin. Blend until smooth. Taste and adjust amounts of lemon juice, salt, and pepper to taste.

Serve this on its own on a bed of arugula with tomatoes slices and kalamata olives or on a platter with Quinoa Tabouli (pg. 68) and whole wheat pita wedges.

Spinach Chickpea Dip

Ingredients

Instructions (serves 4-6)

Ingredients	

1 Tbs olive oil

2 cloves garlic, minced

5 cups spinach, rinsed well and torn into small pieces

1 15 oz can chickpeas

2 Tbs liquid from can of chickpeas

1/4 tsp salt

1/8 tsp freshly ground black pepper

1 Tbs nutritional yeast or vegan parmesan (optional)

IN A LARGE SKILLET, heat oil over medium heat. Add garlic and sauté until fragrant, 2-3 minutes.

Add spinach to pan. When spinach wilts slightly, mix well with garlic. Add chickpeas, liquid from can of chickpeas, salt, and pepper, and sauté for 5-7 minutes. Cool.

Add to blender with nutritional yeast and blend until smooth. Serve with chips, pita triangles, or fresh veggies.

Lettuce Wraps Two Ways

Choose one of these filling and dressing combos to make a quick and healthy dinner, or do one batch of each as an easy appetizer for a party.

Ingredients | Instructions (serves 2-4)

4 large lettuce leaves

2-4 stalks green onions, cleaned very well

Asian filling:

2 carrots, grated

2 stalks green onions, diced small

1 stalk celery, cut in half length-wise and diced small

1 cup shiitake mushrooms, sliced very thin and then diced

1 cup broccoli, diced small

1 cup cauliflower, diced small

Asian dressing:

3 Tbs water

3 Tbs brown rice vinegar

1 Tbs tamari

1 tsp dark sesame oil

1 tsp sugar or agave nectar

1/4 tsp sriracha or other Asian chili sauce

1 cloves of garlic, pressed or minced

COMBINE ALL OF the filling ingredients in a large bowl. In blender, mix all of the dressing ingredients. Toss the filling with half of the dressing and distribute evenly among the four lettuce leaves. Loosely wrap the leaves, careful not to break.

Heat 1-2 cups of water to boil in a large skillet. Next to it, place a bowl of ice water. Separate stalks of green onions and immerse them in the boiling water for 30 seconds to a minute. Take out the stalks and immediately submerge them in the ice water to retain the bright green color and stop the wilting process. Then tie the stalk around the middle of the wrap. Serve immediately with extra dressing in a bowl in the side for dipping if so desired.

Ingredients (continued)

Southwestern filling:

1 can of black beans, drained and rinsed

1 cup frozen corn, thawed and drained

1 large tomato, seeded and diced

1 stalk green onion, diced small

Southwestern dressing:

1/2 of 12 oz package silken firm tofu

1 chipotle peppers in adobo, chopped

1/2 of a ripe avocado

1 Tbs fresh lime juice

salt and pepper to taste / or:

1/2 recipe Tangy Sour Cream (pg. 86)

1 chipotle pepper in adobo, chopped

1/2 of a ripe avocado

Polenta and Eggplant Napoleons

Do not be misled by length of instructions! This colorful appetizer is extremely easy to prepare and features classic flavor combinations that are pleasing to almost every palate.

Most of these steps can be done in advance while preparing for a dinner party, then the assembly can be done in a few minutes while chatting with friends in your kitchen. You can even be drunk and not screw this one up. I promise. Use leftover salsa to make bruschetta with some crusty French bread.

Ingredients

tomato basil salsa:

2 large or 4 roma tomatoes, seeded (see Tips & Techniques, pg. 184) and diced

4 cloves garlic, minced

1/2 cup loosely packed basil leaves, chopped fine

1 tsp olive oil

2 Tbs freshly squeezed lemon juice (about half a lemon)

1 tsp sea salt

1/4 tsp freshly ground black pepper

main ingredients:

1 tube of premade polenta, any flavor

1 skinny medium-sized eggplant

2-3 oz vegan mozzarella, shredded

Instructions (makes 6)

TWO HOURS AHEAD:

Prepare the tomato basil salsa by combining all the ingredients and putting it into the fridge.

Partially peel the eggplant, alternating 1/2" of unpeeled with 1/2" of peeled stripes around the circumference. This helps the eggplant stay intact as it cooks. Slice the eggplant into 1/2-3/4" rounds and salt each slice liberally and then allow them to sit in a colander for an hour.

ONE HOUR AHEAD:

Preheat your oven to 400°. Rinse the eggplant slices very well and then use your hands to gently squeeze the excess water from each slice. Place the slices between two paper towels, pat dry, and then set aside. Spray a cookie sheet with olive oil spray, arrange the eggplant slices on the cookie sheet, spray them with olive oil spray, and then salt and pepper them. Cook them for 15-20 minutes, rotating them once about halfway through.

TEN MINUTES BEFORE SERVING:

Cut open the tube of polenta and slice off twelve 1/4-1/3" slices. Heat a large skillet to medium-high heat and spray with olive oil spray. Reduce the heat to medium and arrange the slices in the skillet. You should be able to fit all twelve, but if not, do them in batches.

Spray the slices with olive oil spray. Sprinkle with a little bit of salt and grind black pepper directly onto the slices. Sauté polenta slices for 4-6 minutes then flip over and sauté for another 5 minutes. Sprinkle a little shredded mozzarella (about 1-2 teaspoons) onto each slice and then cover and continue to sauté until mozz is melted.

Now it's time to stack! Do a slice of eggplant on the bottom, a slice of polenta, a thin layer of tomato basil salsa (try not to use too much juice), another slice of eggplant, another of polenta, and then top it off with a generous rounded heap of salsa. Prepare the rest like this. Serve immediately.

Veggie Wontons with Ginger Miso Dipping Sauce

Ingredients

Instructions (serves 6-8)

24 vegan wonton wrappers

2 tsp peanut oil

2 garlic cloves, minced

2 cups green cabbage, shredded

2 medium or 1/2 cup carrots, shredded

2 green onions, minced

2 tsp soy sauce

dipping sauce:

1/4 cup white miso

1/4 cup mirin

2 Tbs rice vinegar

2 Tbs soy sauce

2 Tbs minced fresh ginger

1 tsp toasted sesame oil

PREHEAT OVEN TO 350°. Coat a large baking sheet with cooking spray. Heat oil in a large skillet over medium-high heat. Reduce to medium and add garlic, cabbage, carrots, and green onions. Sauté until garlic is fragrant and cabbage wilts, 2-4 minutes. Remove from heat and stir in soy sauce.

On a cutting board or clean surface, lay out wonton wrapper. Fill a small bowl with cold water and put next to prep area. Place one spoonful of filling in center of each wrapper. Wet your fingers and moisten the entire circumference of the wonton, then fold over one corner to make a triangle and press edges together to seal. Transfer filled wontons to the sprayed cooking sheet, making sure the wontons aren't touching or they might seal together in the oven.

Bake for 10 minutes; remove the sheet and flip the wontons; bake for another 5-7 minutes or until golden brown and crispy.

Meanwhile, in a blender or food processor, combine ingredients for the dipping sauce and process until well-combined. Transfer to a small bowl and serve with wontons immediately.

Baked Samosas with Cilantro Mint Chutney

I make these when I'm craving Indian food but I don't want all the grease of takeout. This is one of my recipes that is more labor-intensive, so if you want to make it easier on yourself, assemble the samosa filling one night, refrigerate it, transfer the phyllo dough from the freezer to the refrigerator in the morning before work, and then assemble and bake everything when you get home.

Ingredients

1/2 lb (4 or 5) small red potatoes, washed

1 tsp fennel seeds

1 tsp mustard seeds

1 Tbs ground cumin

1/2 tsp turmeric

2 Tbs peanut oil

3 garlic cloves, minced

3 Tbs peeled and grated ginger root

1 yellow onion, diced

1 serrano pepper, minced

1 cup frozen peas, thawed and drained

1 lb fresh spinach, rinsed well, drained, and torn into smaller leaves

salt and pepper to taste

6-8 13"x18" phyllo sheets, thawed

olive oil spray

Instructions (makes 18-24 samosas)

PUT POTATOES IN a pot and fill with enough salted water to cover them. Bring to a boil, then reduce heat and allow them to simmer until tender and easily pierced with a fork, 10-15 minutes. Drain the potatoes, allow them to cool until you can touch them, and then dice them.

In a heavy skillet, dry roast the fennel seeds, mustard seeds, cumin, and turmeric over medium heat, stirring occasionally, until seeds begin to pop, about 2 minutes. Add oil, garlic, ginger, onion, and pepper and sauté, stirring, until onion is soft. Add potatoes, peas, and spinach and sauté, stirring, until spinach is just wilted, about 2-5 minutes. If potato pieces are still a little big, mash them a little with your wooden spoon as you sauté. Season filling with salt and pepper and cool.

Preheat oven to 400°. Lightly grease a baking sheet. Unroll your phyllo sheets and on a large cutting board. Using a sharp knife, cut each phyllo sheet into thirds lengthwise, so each strip is about 6" wide and 13" long.

At the bottom of each strip, use a spoon to put about a tablespoon and a half of filling near one corner. Then fold the other corner over to form a triangle. Continue folding as you would a flag. Use olive oil spray to "seal"

the seam and place the samosa seam down on the baking sheet. Prepare the rest this way until you run out of
filling. Bake for 10 minutes on one side, flip the samosas,
and bake for another 5-8 minutes or until golden brown.
Serve warm with chutney.

CILANTRO MINT CHUTNEY:
1/2 cup packed mint leaves
1/2 cup packed cilantro leaves
1/2 cup packed parsley leaves
2 Tbs fresh lime juice
2" chunk of fresh ginger, peeled and chopped
1-3 slices of canned pickled jalapeño
2 Tbs plain soy yogurt
2 Tbs agave nectar

Using a blender or food processor, combine mint, cilantro, parsley, lime, ginger, and jalapeño and process until
finely chopped. Add soy yogurt and agave nectar and
process until smooth. If necessary, scrape down sides
with a rubber spatula and pulse a few more times. Serve
at room temperature.

Soups

Potato Corn Chowdah

This rich and hearty soup is the solution to the end of summer blues, especially if you can use the fresh corn from the farmers market when it's really cheap but still sweet and delicious!

Ingredients

Instructions (serves 6-8)

2 cups (2-4) yukon gold potatoes

1 cup (1 small) garnet yam

2 medium carrots

1 golden beet (optional)

2 Tbs canola oil

1 small sweet onion, diced

1 celery rib, diced

1 red bell pepper, seeded and diced

2 fresh thyme sprigs

1 cup veggie broth with 1 Tbs cornstarch dissolved in it

1 cup veggie broth

2 cups corn kernels

1 cup soymilk or soy creamer

salt and pepper to taste

PEEL AND ROUGHLY chop the potatoes, yam, carrots, and beets. Heat the oil in a stockpot to medium-high heat. Reduce to medium and add the onion, celery, and red pepper and cook, stirring, until onion is soft. Add roots, leaves from thyme sprigs, and broth with cornstarch. Partially cover and simmer for 30-40 minutes, turning roots over regularly with a wooden spoon, until roots are soft and easily pierced with a fork. Add the rest of the broth and the corn, stir with a wooden spoon, cover, and simmer for another 20 minutes. Remove from heat and stir in soymilk or creamer. Add salt and pepper to taste, but be generous with that salt!

Tortilla Soup

It's pretty much impossible to find a Mexican restaurant that serves vegetarian tortilla soup, and since it's one of my favorite Mexican dishes, I just started making it at home. You can add browned seitan, fake chicken strips, or beans to this if you want extra protein.

Ingredients

3 corn tortillas

1 medium red bell pepper

1 tsp canola oil

2 cloves garlic, minced

1 cup veggie broth

1 stalk celery, diced

1 small yellow onion, diced

4 cups veggie broth

1 cup fresh or frozen corn kernels, thawed

1 chile pepper, deseeded and minced

1 tsp cumin

1/2 tsp paprika

1/2 tsp salt

1/2 tsp black pepper

1/4 tsp thyme

1/8 tsp cayenne

1/2 cup or one roma tomato, diced

1 ripe avocado, diced

lime wedges, chopped cilantro, and cubed avocado for garnish

Instructions (serves 4-6)

SET OVEN ON broil and move topmost oven rack to one of the top slots (you will be putting red pepper in the oven and the top of the pepper should be about 6 inches from the heat coil). Brush tortillas on both sides with thin layer of olive oil, or spray. Cut the tortillas in half and then into strips and place on cookie sheet. Place red pepper on cookie sheet with tortilla.

Place tortillas and pepper in oven and watch carefully, ready to pull out at any second. When tortillas start to brown and crisp up, pull out, remove from cookie sheet, and set them aside, returning red pepper to oven. Rotate pepper until it is black on all sides, 30-60 seconds or so on each side, and then take it out and turn off oven.

Place pepper into a sealable plastic bag immediately and allow pepper to "sweat" for 10 minutes or so. Take pepper out and peel off the blackened skin, then cut in half and remove seeds. Cut pepper into thin strips.

In pot, heat oil to medium-high. Reduce to medium and add garlic. After a minute, add 1 cup of broth to pot along with celery and onion. Cook until vegetables are soft, 5-8 minutes. Add the rest of the broth. Add tortillas, strips of red pepper, corn, chile pepper, and spices. Bring to a quick boil and then reduce heat to medium-low, cover, and simmer for 5-10 minutes.

Add tomato and avocado to the soup. Stir in well. Reduce to low, cover again, and cook for 10 more minutes. Serve immediately with recommended garnishes.

Black Bean Soup

This is the only black bean soup recipe you'll ever need. Try it once as written and then adjust the variables to suit your tastes: one more chili pepper for extra spiciness; half the lime juice if you want it less tangy; the whole soup blended if you like it really creamy. But all the variables for the perfect black bean soup are already here.

Ingredients

2 cups dry black beans

2 Tbs baking soda

4 cups water

2 bay leaves or 1" piece of kombu

1 tsp kosher or sea salt

1 Tbs olive oil

1 large red onion, diced

1 rib of celery, diced

1 red bell pepper, seeded and chopped

1/2 tsp salt

4-6 cloves garlic, minced

1 Tbs cumin

1 chipotle chile, minced

1 tsp adobo sauce from chipotles

1 tsp liquid smoke

4 cups veggie broth

juice from one large lime

Instructions (serves 6-10)

SOAK BEANS OVERNIGHT in 4 cups of water with baking soda. Drain but don't rinse. Place beans, bay leaves, 4 cups of water, and salt in large pot. Bring to boil over medium-high heat. Use a ladle to skim the gray scum off the surface, reduce heat to low, cover, and simmer until beans are tender, 45-60 minutes. Take off the heat and fish out the bay leaves. Set aside.

In a 2 quart pot, heat oil on medium-high heat. Reduce heat to medium, add onion, celery, and bell pepper and cook until vegetables are tender and browning, 8-10 minutes, stirring occasionally. Reduce heat to medium-low and add salt, garlic and cumin and cook for 3-5 more minutes, stirring frequently. Stir in beans, bean cooking liquid, chipotle chiles, adobo sauce, liquid smoke and broth. Increase heat to medium-high and bring to boil, then reduce heat to low and simmer, uncovered, stirring occasionally, about 30 minutes.

Ladle the scum off the the surface of the soup. Transfer 4 ladlefuls of broth only and 2 ladlefuls of beans only to the food processor or blender, process until smooth, and return to pot. Alternately, use a handheld blender to partially blend the soup in the pot. Stir in lime juice. Serve immediately with desired garnishes. Garnish with any of the following: cubed avocado, a dollop of Tangy Sour Cream (pg. 86), diced tomatoes, cilantro leaves.

Miso Soup with Edamame

Because boiling miso removes all of its nutrients, you cook the vegetables separately from the miso broth and add them at the end. If you're a tofu freak, you can add 1/2" cubes of raw tofu at the end. I myself am merely a tofu enthusiast, and feel that the edamame provides enough protein for the soup.

Ingredients

1 quart water

2 Tbs miso paste

1 tsp peanut oil

4 oz shiitake or oyster mushrooms, destemmed and sliced thin

1 cup sugar peas, sliced in half diagonally

1 cup shelled edamame

1/2 cup scallions

1/4 cup diced lemongrass (optional)

1/4 cup sake (optional)

1/2-1 tsp Asian chili paste or sauce

bean sprouts for garnish (optional)

Instructions (serves 4)

IN A POT, mix miso with water and bring to a low simmer. In a wok or large nonstick skillet, heat peanut oil to medium-high heat. Add mushrooms and sugar peas and sauté for 1-2 minutes. Add edamame and scallions. Sauté for another minute or two. Mix in lemongrass and sake and sauté for another couple of minutes, stirring frequently, until sake reduces.

Transfer vegetables to miso broth. Stir in Asian chili paste and remove from heat. Serve immediately, garnished with bean sprouts.

Black Eyed Pea Soup

I came up with this soup when I was sick and wanted something nutritious, filling, easy, and I wouldn't get tired of it by the end of the day. It turned out to be one of my boyfriend's and my favorite soups ever, and now I crave it on every cold and rainy day in Portland. We have a lot of cold and rainy days in Portland.

Ingredients

1 cup dried black eyed peas

2 Tbs olive oil

4 cloves garlic, minced

1 yellow onion, diced

2 stalks celery, diced

4 cups veggie broth or water

4 medium yukon gold potatoes, or about 2 cups, peeled and cut into 1" chunks

1/4 cup fresh dill, chopped

1 tsp thyme

1/4 cup nutritional yeast

generous amounts of salt and freshly ground black pepper

Instructions (serves 6, or you all day when you're sick)

RINSE BLACK EYED PEAS and then soak for 8 hours or overnight. Drain and rinse.

In a large stockpot, heat olive oil on medium heat. Add garlic and sauté for a minute or two. Add onion and celery and sauté until soft. Add veggie broth, rinsed black eyed peas, potato chunks, and herbs. Bring to a boil and then reduce to a simmer and cover.

Cook for one hour or until both peas and potatoes are tender. Potatoes should break apart if you pierce them with a fork. Turn off the heat and stir in nutritional yeast. Add salt and pepper to taste at the table at time of serving.

Curried Carrot Ginger Soup

This simple soup has huge taste and half the fat of most curried soups, which typically use a whole can of coconut milk. It is still more fatty than most of my dishes, so I only make it about once a month and then just fantasize about it for the rest of the month. February is easier.

Serve this on its own at lunch or as a precursor to an Indian dinner to set the flavor.

Ingredients

1 Tbs olive oil

2-3 cloves or 1 Tbs garlic, minced

2 tsp curry powder

3 Tbs fresh ginger, minced

1/2 medium yellow onion, chopped

1 lb or 6-8 medium carrots, peeled and chopped

3 1/2 cups veggie broth

2 bay leaves

1/2 cup light coconut milk

1/4 cup chopped cilantro for garnish

salt to taste

Instructions (makes 4 servings)

HEAT OIL IN a saucepan over medium heat. Add the garlic and curry powder and sauté until garlic is fragrant. Add the ginger and onions, mix well, and sauté for another 2-3 minutes. Add carrots, broth, and bay leaves. Bring to a boil and then reduce the heat, cover, and simmer for 20-30 minutes or until carrots are tender. Fish out the bay leaves. Working in batches with a food processor or blender, or using an immersion blender, blend soup until smooth. Stir in coconut milk. Garnish with cilantro before serving. Salt at the table to taste.

Mom's Lentil Soup

This is a version of the lentil soup my mom makes. I am not exaggerating when I say it's the greatest lentil soup ever. Try it if you don't believe me.

This freezes well, which is good to know because it makes a boatload. When you reheat the leftovers, add 1/4 cup of water or so per serving, as the soup tends to absorb the broth when it's chilling in the fridge or freezer.

Ingredients

2 Tbs non-hydrogenated margarine

2 cloves garlic, minced

1 large yellow onion, diced

2 carrots, peeled and diced

2 ribs of celery, halved lengthwise and then diced*

6 cups veggie broth or water

2 bay leaves

1 1/2 cups dry brown or LePuy lentils

1 28 oz can diced tomatoes

1/2 tsp thyme

1/8 tsp ground cloves

1/2 cup red wine

liberal amount of salt

freshly ground black pepper to taste

1/4 cup parsley, chopped fine

*What you're looking for here is a traditional mirepoix, which is a ratio of onions, carrots, and celery at 2:1:1. So if this amount of ingredients doesn't give you that ratio (or near enough), adjust.

Instructions (makes 8-12 servings)

HEAT MARGARINE ON medium-low in largest stock pot you own. Add the garlic and sauté for a minute or two or until garlic is fragrant. Add onion, carrots, and celery, coating the vegetables well, and sauté for 8-10 minutes or so.

Add veggie broth, bay leaves, lentils, and a little salt and pepper to pot. Bring soup to a boil and then immediately reduce heat to low simmer and cover the pot. Allow to simmer, covered, for 40 minutes. Stir every 10 minutes or so.

Take half the can of tomatoes and blend them well in a blender or food processor. Add diced tomatoes, blended tomatoes, and thyme to pot at the same time. Mix well, cover again, and continue to simmer for another 20 minutes.

Finally, remove soup from heat. Fish out the bay leaves. If you prefer the soup to be more creamy than hearty, transfer half of the soup to a blender or food processor and blend smooth and then fold it back in with the rest of the soup. Stir in cloves, red wine, and salt and pepper to taste. Just before serving, stir in parsley.

Salads

Daily Green Salads

At my house, we eat our salads on dinner plates and our dinners on salad plates.

IF YOU HAVEN'T experimented much with making your own dressings, it's mind-blowingly easy and much cheaper than buying bottled dressings. Vinaigrettes are just oil and vinegar in a 2:1 ratio with some salt and pepper, sometimes also with fresh lemon juice and a little sweetener—and a tiny bit of Dijon mustard for the balsamic vinaigrettes. For herbed vinaigrettes, mince in 1-2 Tbs of fresh parsley, dill, or cilantro. If you like your dressings more creamy, throw it in the blender with a little silken tofu. There's a store-bought salad dressing that you really love? Why not read the ingredients on the back and try making it at home? You might be able to recreate the taste with less fat, preservatives, and sugar than the packaged version, and fresher is always better—better tasting and better for you.

These are some of our favorite green salad combinations:

» bite-size pieces of kale and swiss chard marinated for 2-4 hours in a dressing of fresh lemon juice, olive oil, sesame seeds, and salt and pepper, and then slivers of red onion, avocado, cherry tomatoes, and raw sunflower seeds thrown in just before serving

» yellow, red, and green heirloom tomatoes sliced thin and drizzled with a cider vinaigrette on a bed of arugula or baby spinach

» mixed spring greens with dried cranberries, figs, and walnuts and tossed with a balsamic vinaigrette

» torn romaine lettuce with pink grapefruit, slices of tart apple, and celery with a citrus and grapeseed oil dressing

Antipasto Salad

This is a great precursor to an Italian or Mediterranean meal.

Ingredients

Instructions (serves 3-5)

2 hearts of romaine, cleaned very well and torn by hand

1/2 cup flat-leafed parsley, leaves only

2 ribs of celery, halved lengthwise and then sliced at an angle

1/4 cup chopped jarred roasted red peppers

4-6 canned artichoke hearts, quartered then roughly chopped

1/2 cup kalamata or spanish olives, halved

1/2 pint grape or cherry tomatoes, halved

1/2 large or 1 small red onion, quartered and sliced thinly

dressing:

5 Tbs pesto (if frozen, bring to room temperature)

2 Tbs red wine vinegar

COMBINE ALL SALAD ingredients in a large bowl. Whisk dressing ingredients, pour over salad, and toss well to coat. Serve immediately.

Taco Salad

I usually make this for lunch as a full meal but have also doubled it and brought it to potlucks and seen it devoured by adults and kids, omnivores and grateful vegans alike. If you serve the salad with vegan sour cream (like the Tangy Sour Cream) and mush it in with the seasoned TVP, it gets so creamy and savory that you'll salivate just thinking about it, kind of like I am now.

Ingredients

Instructions (serves 2-4 as a full meal)

taco seasoning:

1 Tbs chili powder

2 tsp onion powder

1 tsp cumin

1 tsp garlic powder

1 tsp paprika

1 tsp oregano

1 tsp sugar or 1/4 tsp Stevia Plus

1/2 tsp sea salt

Mix all ingredients together.

main ingredients:

1 cup TVP

7/8 cup veggie broth or water

1 recipe taco seasoning

2 Tbs organic ketchup

1 small head romaine lettuce, rinsed very well, patted or spun dry, and shredded

BRING BROTH TO boil in saucepot. Reduce heat to low and add TVP to broth, mixing until broth is fully absorbed. Add the taco seasoning and ketchup and mix well and continue to heat for another ten minutes or so. Keep on burner on lowest setting until ready to assemble salad.

Arrange on a plate in layers in this order: the lettuce; tomatoes; kidney beans; seasoned TVP; sour cream; avocado; black olives. If you haven't used sour cream, you'll want to drizzle on 2-3 tablespoons of your favorite salad dressing.

Ingredients (continued)

1 medium tomato diced or 1 cup grape or cherry tomatoes, halved

1 15 oz can kidney beans, drained and rinsed

1/2 avocado, cubed (optional)

1/4 cup sliced black olives (optional)

1/4 cup Tangy Sour Cream (pg. 86) or 3 Tbs fat free or low fat dressing of your choice

Photo: Katie Marggraf

Minty Summer Fruit Salad

Don't tell the vegan police but I'm not a big fruit fan. However, when summer rolls around and the farmers market is packed to the gills with berries, there is nothing I want more than to cart it all home and live off giant fruit salads. After a few hours in the fridge, the color from the berries will dye the rest of the salad a very pleasing pinky-purple color. Good luck making it last that long.

Ingredients

2-3 ripe bananas, sliced

1 cup strawberries, sliced

1 cup raspberries, blackberries, or marionberries

1 cup blueberries

2 peaches, pitted and diced

dressing:

juice of 1 small orange

juice of 1 large lime

1/2 cup mint leaves, shredded

Instructions (makes a lot!)

ADD FRUIT AND berries to a big bowl. Lightly toss so fruit juices mix. Then add dressing.

Toss well. Serve immediately or allow to chill in fridge for a few hours.

- -

TROPICAL FRUIT SALAD: Replace berries and peaches with chopped mangoes, pineapple chunks, and peeled and sliced kiwis.

Barley and Avocado Salad

A simple and delicious salad that complements pretty much any meal. If you're eating it on its own, you might want to add chickpeas or cubes of sautéed tofu for a more well-rounded dish.

Ingredients

Instructions (makes 4-6 servings)

3 cups vegetable broth

1 cup pearl barley

2 ripe avocados, cubed

1/2 large red onion, diced

1/4 cup oil-packed sun-dried tomatoes, diced

2 Tbs fresh basil, chopped

2 packed cups arugula, baby spinach, or mixed greens (optional)

dressing:

3 Tbs balsamic vinegar

1 Tbs olive oil

1 Tbs sun-dried tomato oil

1/2 tsp Dijon mustard

pinch each salt and pepper

IN MEDIUM SAUCEPAN, bring vegetable broth to a boil. Add barley and return to boil. Reduce heat to low, cover and cook 45 minutes or until barley is tender and liquid is absorbed. Transfer to medium bowl and allow to cool.

When completely cool, add avocados, onion, sun-dried tomatoes, and basil. Combine dressing ingredients in a lidded jar and shake very well to emulsify (see Glossary, pg. 185), then pour over salad and mix with a wooden spoon. Serve immediately on its own or on a bed of greens.

If preparing this well in advance of serving, don't cut and add avocados until the last minute. Everything else can be combined and will develop stronger flavors the longer it sits in the fridge.

Texas Caviar

Obviously, I'm a little biased towards Texas Caviar, although I don't remember ever hearing it called this when I was growing up in Texas. It was just my favorite bean salad, ubiquitous at barbecues and church potlucks, never made at home by my Yank parents, which probably only added to its appeal. Recipes vary greatly and this is my take on it: the addition of black beans, fresh herbs, and just a little bit of sweetness to offset the tang.

Ingredients

Instructions (serves 6-8)

2 15 oz cans black eyed peas, drained and rinsed

1 15 oz can black beans, drained and rinsed

1 bunch green onions, thinly sliced

1/2 cup fresh parsley, chopped

1/4 cup packed cilantro leaves, chopped

2 Tbs olive oil

2 Tbs red wine vinegar

juice from medium lime

1/2 tsp juice from jalapeño jar

1/2 tsp agave nectar

1 clove garlic, minced

1 pickled jalapeño, chopped

1/4 tsp sea salt

1/8 tsp cumin

dash cayenne pepper

COMBINE BLACK EYED PEAS, black beans, green onions, parsley, and cilantro in a large bowl. In a smaller bowl, briskly whisk together the oil, vinegar, and lime juice until it emulsifies (see Glossary, pg. 185). Add jalapeño juice, agave nectar, garlic, jalapeño, salt, and cumin and whisk again until well-combined. Add dressing to salad and use a wooden spoon to mix the salad. Sprinkle a dash of cayenne pepper on the top and stir again. Refrigerate for at least one hour to allow flavors to fully blend. Serve at room temperature.

Photo: Katie Marggraf

Goddess Pasta Salad

If you have a potluck or a barbecue coming up, try this salad, which comes together quickly, refrigerates and travels well, and feeds a boatload. Creamy and tangy, this pasta salad is a great alternative to the deli-style, mayonnaise-laden macaroni salad.

Ingredients

Instructions (makes at least 10 hearty servings)

3 Tbs sesame seeds

1 lb dry multigrain small pasta, preferably a tube pasta like penne

1 pint cherry tomatoes, halved, or whole grape tomatoes

1 large cucumber, peeled in stripes, quartered lengthwise, and sliced

1 cup frozen shelled edamame, steamed

1 cup frozen sweet corn, steamed

3 stalks green onion, sliced into thin rounds

3 Tbs vegan mayonnaise

sea salt to taste

dressing:

2 cloves garlic

1 stalk green onion, chopped

1 Tbs fresh parsley

1 Tbs fresh dill

1/2 tsp salt

6 oz lite firm silken tofu

2 Tbs tahini

PREHEAT OVEN TO 450°. Spread sesame seeds on a cookie sheet in a thin layer. Toast until seeds begin to pop, usually 5 minutes or so.

Cook pasta according to directions on package in salted water. Allow pasta to drain before transferring to a very large bowl.

Steam the edamame and corn if you haven't already. Drain.

In a blender or food processor, blend first the garlic, green onion, parsley, dill, and salt until they are chopped fine. Add the rest of the dressing ingredients and blend until smooth.

Add the dressing to the pasta and use a wooden spoon to mix very well, so the dressing gets inside of the pasta a little. Add cherry tomatoes, cucumbers, edamame, corn, and green onion and mix again. Finally add the mayonnaise, toasted sesame seeds, and sea salt to taste and mix one more time. Serve at room temperature or chilled.

Ingredients (continued)

2 Tbs water

2 Tbs fresh lemon juice

1 Tbs rice vinegar

1 tsp apple cider vinegar

1 tsp tamari or soy sauce

1 tsp toasted sesame oil

pinch freshly ground black pepper

Photo: Jen Oaks

Couscous Chickpea Salad

I really wanted to like couscous, but almost every recipe I tried was either dead boring, tasteless, or way too fatty to be considered a salad. So I came up with this salad—one of those great salads that tastes even better with every passing day in the fridge—and I'm finally ready to say that I love couscous!

Ingredients

1 cup whole wheat couscous

1/2 tsp salt

1 1/2 cups cooked or 1 15 oz can of chickpeas, drained and rinsed

1/4 cup parsley, minced

2 stalks green onions, sliced into thin rounds

1 Tbs olive oil

2 cloves garlic, minced

1 leek, cleaned extremely well and then cut into thin rounds

4 oz or about 1 cup cremini mushrooms, sliced thin

dressing:

2 tsp grapeseed oil or olive oil

2 Tbs red wine vinegar

1 Tbs balsamic vinegar

2 Tbs lemon juice or juice of one medium lemon

2 cloves garlic, pressed or minced

salt and pepper to taste

Instructions (serves 4-6)

MIX 1 1/2 CUPS boiling water and 1/2 teaspoon salt with couscous in large bowl. Cover with a dish towel, plate, or plastic wrap to seal in and let sit for 5-10 minutes. Fluff with a fork. Add chickpeas, parsley, and green onions and mix well.

Heat the olive oil in a large skillet over medium heat. Add minced garlic and leeks and sauté until leeks begin to turn brown (but are still mostly bright green and yellow). Add mushrooms to skillet and sauté for another 2-3 minutes, until mushrooms just begin to brown. Turn off the heat and allow to cool. Add leek and mushroom mixture to couscous and chickpeas.

In a small bowl, whisk dressing ingredients. Toss dressing with salad. Add salt and pepper to taste. Serve immediately or chill first.

Quinoa Tabouli

Forget your greasy tabouli recipes. This is a lot fresher-tasting and I don't have to tell you about the miracle of quinoa, do I?

Ingredients

3/4 cup quinoa

1 tbs olive oil

2 medium or 3 roma tomatoes, seeded (see Tips & Techniques, pg. tips184) and diced

6 green onions, whitish-green parts only, sliced thinly

3 garlic cloves, minced

1 bunch of parsley, leaves only, chopped fine

1/3-1/2 cup of mint leaves, chopped fine

2 large limes

salt and freshly ground black pepper to taste

Instructions (serves 4-6)

RINSE QUINOA IN a fine mesh strainer under cold water for a minute or so. If you don't have a fine mesh strainer, you can use a coffee filter. Add quinoa to a pot with 3/4 cup of water and bring to a boil. Reduce to low, cover, and simmer for about 10 minutes or until water is fully absorbed, checking every few minutes. Take quinoa off the heat and add to a large bowl. Stir the olive oil into the quinoa, fluffing up the grain as you incorporate the oil. Allow to cool for 10 minutes.

Meanwhile, combine the tomatoes, green onions, garlic, parsley, and mint in a medium bowl.

When quinoa is room temperature, add contents of medium bowl and stir well. Squeeze the limes directly into the salad and mix well. Add salt and pepper to taste. You can eat this immediately but it tastes even better after it's been refrigerated for a few hours.

Carrot Salad with Herb Lime Dressing

This recipe is really perfect for when you have to buy a whole bag of carrots for another recipe but you use only one or two. Here's a way to use those up before they become shriveled in your vegetable crisper.

Ingredients

Instructions (serves 4-6)

6-8 medium carrots, peeled (about 4 cups when grated)

1/2 cup golden raisins (optional)

dressing:

1 Tbs olive oil

2 Tbs fresh lime juice (about half a large lime)

1 tsp agave nectar

1/2 tsp salt

2 Tbs chopped cilantro

1 Tbs chopped parsley

GRATE THE CARROTS either by hand or with a food processor. Set aside. In a blender or with a whisk, combine dressing ingredients and toss with the carrots. Add raisins and toss again.

Wild Rice Salad

I came up with this recipe when I was broke and running out of fresh produce! This isn't an everyday salad due to the fat content but it's so easy and delicious that I love to whip it out every once in a while. Try it warm, room temperature, or chilled to see which way you like it best. I kind of like it two days old, at 11 PM, eating it with a fork straight out of the bowl with the refrigerator door open.

Ingredients

1 cup wild rice or wild rice blend

2 cups veggie broth

2 tsp olive oil

1 Tbs lemon juice

1/3 cup (8-10) pitted kalamata olives

1/4 cup sundried tomatoes packed in oil

1 small can of artichoke hearts, drained

salt to taste

Instructions (serves 2-4 as a main dish, 4-6 as a side)

COMBINE WILD RICE and broth in a pot and bring to a boil. Reduce heat, cover, and simmer for 30 minutes or until water is fully absorbed. Fluff the rice with a fork before transferring to a bowl.

Add the oil and lemon juice to the rice and mix well.

Rinse the olives and sundried tomatoes in a strainer under cold water. Blot with a paper towel and cut the olives in half and slice the tomatoes into strips and then in half. Quarter each artichoke. Add olives, tomatoes, and artichokes to the salad and toss well. Starting at around 1/2 teaspoon, add salt until the flavor is perfect for you.

Sauces, Salsas, and Toppings

Sundried Tomato Cream Sauce

 (serves 2-4)

2 tsp non-hydrogenated margarine

2 cloves garlic, minced

1 cup soymilk or soy creamer

1 Tbs cornstarch

2 sundried tomatoes packed in oil, rinsed and patted dry

1 Tbs sherry or dry white wine

1/2 tsp thyme

1 tsp chopped fresh dill or rosemary or 1/2 tsp dry

1/2 tsp salt

pinch freshly ground black pepper

SAUTÉ GARLIC IN MARGARINE in a (preferably nonstick) saucepot for 2-3 minutes over medium-high heat. Combine soymilk and cornstarch in a small bowl or glass and use a fork or whisk to mix well until cornstarch is completely dissolved, with no clumps. Add soymilk mixture to the saucepan and whisk slowly for a few minutes.

While sauce thickens a little, slice sundried tomatoes into thin strips and then chop them and add them to soymilk mixture. Add sherry, herbs, salt, and pepper, and simmer for a few minutes, continuing to whisk. Reduce heat to low and continue to whisk for another few minutes as sauce thickens more. Turn off the heat.

If you have an immersion blender, blend the sauce right in the saucepan. I hope you're wearing an apron. If not, allow it to cool a little and then transfer to a blender or food processor.

Serve immediately.

Ratatouille Pasta Sauce

I love the vegetables and flavors in traditional ratatouille, but I find it a bit boring on its own, so I've turned it into a chunky pasta sauce. This works best with a hearty pasta like penne or farfalle.

Ingredients

Instructions (serves 4-6)

1 eggplant

2 zucchini

1 summer squash

1/2 yellow onion

olive oil and balsamic vinegar for roasting

large granule sea salt or kosher salt

2 Tbs olive oil

2 cloves minced garlic

1 lb or 3-4 medium tomatoes, chopped

1/2 tsp salt

1/4 cup fresh basil, choppped

1 Tbs fresh rosemary, chopped

1/2 tsp oregano

15 oz tomato sauce, no salt added

1/4 tsp crushed red pepper flakes

additional salt to taste

PREHEAT OVEN TO 425°. Spray a large roasting pan or cookie sheet with nonstick cooking spray.

Slice eggplant in thirds lengthwise. Slice zucchini and summer squash in half lengthwise. Arrange cut side up in one layer, along with the half onion, in roasting pan and brush with olive oil and sprinkle with salt.

Roast for 15 minutes. Remove from oven, drizzle or brush with balsamic vinegar, and return veggies to oven. Roast until vinegar is evaporated, 3-5 minutes. Remove from oven and allow to cool for 10 minutes or until vegetables are cool to touch. Cut roasted veggies into about 3/4" cubes for the eggplant and squash and bite-size pieces for the onion.

In a large stock pot, heat 2 tablespoons of olive oil over low heat. Add garlic and allow the garlic to sweat (see Glossary, pg. 185), covered, for 6-10 minutes. Add tomatoes and salt, mix with garlic, cover again, and allow to sweat for another 5 minutes or so. Add roasted veggies, basil, rosemary, and oregano, cover again, and continue to sweat for 40 minutes.

Uncover, add tomato sauce and red pepper flakes, stir well, and allow sauce to sit on the stove on the lowest possible heat as you prepare your pasta according to the directions on the package.

Serve warm with a ratio of 1:1 pasta sauce to pasta. Add additional salt at the table to taste, if necessary.

Marinara

Ingredients

Instructions (makes 2-3 cups)

1 Tbs olive oil

1 medium yellow onion, diced

6 garlic cloves, minced

1/2-3/4 tsp red pepper flakes

1 28 oz can diced tomatoes, with juices

1 15 oz can tomato sauce

1 tsp sugar

1 tsp dried oregano

1/2 cup lightly packed fresh basil leaves, chiffonaded

1/4 cup fresh parsley, chopped

salt and freshly ground black pepper

HEAT OIL IN large (preferably cast iron) skillet over medium heat. Add onion and sauté until just tender. Add garlic and crushed red pepper and sauté for 5 minutes or so. Stir in tomatoes. Cover and simmer for 10 minutes. Add tomato sauce, sugar, oregano, basil and parsley. Stir well and then cover and simmer another 10 minutes. Uncover and simmer until thickened, about 5 minutes, stirring every minute or so. If sauce is getting too thick, thin it out with 1/4-1/2 cup water. Season with salt and pepper to taste but be careful not to overdo it. Transfer majority of the sauce to blender or food processor and blend a bit, then mix back in with rest of marinara. Serve immediately.

MUSHROOM MARINARA: Add 8 oz sliced button mushrooms at the same time you add the garlic and red pepper; reduce basil to 1/4 cup.

PUTTANESCA MARINARA: Add 1/4 cup drained capers and 1/2 cup black olives, sliced in half at the same time you add the tomatoes; reduce basil to 1/4 cup.

Béchamel Sauce

This simple white sauce is delicious alone on noodles with grilled or sautéed veggies (particularly mushrooms), or use it to make cream sauces for other pasta dishes.

Ingredients

Instructions (makes 2 cups)

2 Tbs non-hydrogenated margarine

1/4 cup shallots, minced

3 Tbs unbleached all purpose flour

2 cups soymilk

1/2 teaspoon salt

1/8 tsp nutmeg

1/8 tsp ground white pepper

MELT MARGARINE IN a large, heavy-bottomed saucepan over medium heat. Add shallots and sauté 2-4 minutes, until tender.

Add flour 1 tablespoon at a time and whisk until there are no lumps. Reduce heat to low and briskly whisk for one minute. Slowly whisk in soymilk and bring to a simmer. Reduce heat to medium-low and simmer for 10 minutes, whisking for 10 seconds out of every minute as sauce thickens.

Whisk in salt, nutmeg, and pepper and take sauce off the heat. Allow to cool very slightly before serving, 5 minutes or so.

HERBED BÉCHAMEL: Add 1 Tbs each fresh chopped tarragon and thyme with seasonings at the end.

Pesto

I am a sucker for pesto, which is why there are three pesto recipes in this book. This is a way to make it without using much oil, and I've added spinach not only to keep the colors bright but to add extra vitamins. I'm packing vitamins into your diet without your permission.

Don't just pigeonhole pesto as a pasta sauce. Add pesto to your tofu scramble, to polenta, or use it as a spread for a sandwich of grilled marinated veggies. One of my favorite snacks is to spread a little on a slice of pita bread and broil it in the oven.

Ingredients

Instructions (makes 8-12 servings)

3 Tbs pine nuts

2 oz or 2 cups loosely packed basil, leaves only

1 cup packed baby spinach leaves

3-4 cloves garlic, crushed

2 Tbs vegan parmesan (pg. 100) or nutritional yeast (optional)

1/2-3/4 tsp salt

1 Tbs olive oil

1-2 Tbs fresh lemon juice

1/4-1/3 cup vegetable broth

TOAST PINE NUTS in a single layer in a toaster oven or oven at 400° until they're brown. Watch carefully as this won't take very long and you don't want them to burn.

Add toasted pine nuts, basil, spinach, garlic, vegan parmesan, and salt to food processor, begin to process, and add olive oil while processing. Stop and use plastic spatula to scrape down the sides if necessary.

Add lemon juice and process. While processing, add broth slowly in a stream and stop when consistency is somewhere between a paste and a sauce, no more than 1/3 cup.

Serve immediately or store pesto in compartments in ice cube trays for easy storage and portion control, thawing one cube at a time as needed.

Mexican Pesto

Okay, you might not actually find pesto served anywhere in Mexico, but this is what it would taste like if you did. I love this fresh and light sauce over capellini pasta or added to a tofu scramble with avocados.

Ingredients

Instructions

1/4 cup roasted pumpkin seeds

1/8 cup shelled pistachios

2 cloves garlic

2 cups cilantro, packed

1/2 cup parsley, packed

half a large lime

1/4-1/2 tsp salt

tiny dash cayenne pepper

1 Tbs olive oil

1 Tbs grapeseed oil

2 Tbs water

IN A FOOD PROCESSOR or heavy-duty blender, process pumpkin seeds, pistachios, garlic, cilantro, and parsley until it's a fine paste. Add lime juice, salt, and pepper, and pulse a few more times. While processor is running, slowly add oils in a thin stream. Turn it off and use a rubber spatula to scrape down the sides. Put the top back on and run the processor again and slowly add the water.

Serve immediately or store pesto in compartments in ice cube trays for easy storage and portion control, thawing one cube at a time as needed.

Lemon Artichoke Pesto

Ingredients

Instructions (makes about 2 cups)

4 garlic cloves

1/4 cup almonds

1 15 oz can artichoke hearts, drained

1 cup parsley

1/4 cup lemon juice

1 Tbs olive oil

1/2 tsp sea salt

1/2 tsp red pepper flakes

1/4 cup veggie broth

2 Tbs vegan parmesan (pg. 100)

IN A FOOD PROCESSOR or blender, pulse garlic and almonds until chopped. Add artichoke hearts and process again until blended. Add parsley, lemon juice, oil, salt, and pepper, and process until well-mixed. With the processor or blender running, slowly add broth in a stream. Add parmesan and pulse a few more times until mixed in.

Serve immediately or transfer to storage.

Mushroom Gravy

This quick and versatile mushroom gravy can be served over mashed potatoes, Kasha Varnishkes (pg. 146), udon noodles, or just veggies and brown rice.

Ingredients

2 large garlic cloves, minced

1 tsp olive oil

1 shallot or 1/2 a sweet yellow onion, cut into thin slivers

1 1/2 cups mixed mushrooms (any combination of shiitake, button, oyster, morel), sliced thinly

2 tsp soy sauce

1/4 cup dry white wine or cooking sherry

2 tsp cornstarch dissolved in 1 cup cold water

1 Tbs fresh lemon juice

2 Tbs fresh parsley leaves, minced

salt and freshly ground black pepper

Instructions (makes 2 servings)

IN A HEAVY SKILLET over medium heat, sauté garlic in olive oil until fragrant. Add shallot and cook, stirring, until softened and translucent, 8-10 minutes. Add mushrooms and soy sauce and sauté mixture over medium-high heat, stirring, until mushrooms begin to brown, 2-5 minutes.

Add wine and simmer, stirring, for a minute or two. Stir cornstarch mixture and add to skillet. Bring mixture to a boil, stirring, and simmer 2 minutes. Reduce heat to low and stir while gravy thickens. Stir in lemon juice and parsley and season gravy with salt and pepper. Serve immediately or blend it first if you like a more creamy gravy.

MUSHROOM STROGANOFF: Add 2 Tbs unbleached all purpose flour and 1 cup of soymilk in place of cornstarch and water. Serve over noodles.

Almond Milk Gravy

Yum. Sometimes I make this really salty and serve it on toast, and it tastes a whole lot like the cream chipped beef that my mom made when I was growing up, but mostly this is my default gravy for biscuits and gravy.

You can substitute any nondairy milk for the almond milk if it's not your thing, but I love the sweet and slightly nutty flavor it adds, and find it indispensable.

Ingredients

1/2 cup almond milk

2 Tbs unbleached all purpose flour

1 Tbs olive oil

6-8 oz low fat vegetarian sausage, crumbled

1 Tbs non-hydrogenated margarine

1 cup almond milk

plenty of freshly ground black pepper

salt to taste

Instructions (serves 4)

IN A LIDDED JAR, combine 1/2 cup almond milk and flour and shake vigorously. Set aside.

In a large, heavy-bottomed skillet, heat oil to medium-high. Crumble in sausage and reduce heat to medium. Sauté sausage crumbles until they're evenly brown, breaking the bits up a bit with a wooden spoon as you stir, about 6-8 minutes. Using a slotted spoon, transfer sausage to a bowl or plate.

Heat margarine in skillet until melted and reduce heat to medium-low. Give the lidded jar with the almond milk and flour another good shake, then open and pour the mixture into the skillet in a steady stream while slowly whisking. Add remaining cup of almond milk a little bit at a time, continuing to whisk, as gravy thickens, for 5-8 minutes. Add sausage back to the gravy.

Season with plenty of freshly ground black pepper, but taste before adding any salt, as sausage is salty.

Gravy can be served immediately or left in the skillet on lowest heat to thicken more until ready to serve.

Lemon Tahini Dressing

My testers went so nutso over this dressing, you would have thought that I had invented tahini myself based on their reactions. One even said that it was: "perfection in every way." See for yourself if you agree.

Ingredients

Instructions (makes about 1 1/2 cups or 12 servings)

1/2 cup water

1/2 cup tahini

1/3 cup plain soy yogurt

juice from two large lemons

3 garlic cloves

2 Tbs olive oil

2 Tbs fresh parsley

1/2 tsp sea salt

1/2 tsp cumin

1/8 tsp paprika

1/8 tsp freshly ground black pepper

COMBINE ALL INGREDIENTS and blend until completely smooth and well mixed. For a variation, use roasted garlic cloves. Serve over braised cauliflower (pg. 105), steamed broccoli, greens, or to replace tzatziki sauce for falafel sandwiches.

Creamy Pepita Dressing

This spicy dressing is delicious drizzled on a green salad to prepare the palate for a homemade Mexican meal, or you can make the dip variation to serve with a platter of crudités.

Ingredients

1/4 cup raw pumpkin seeds

1 Tbs tamari

2 tsp olive oil

4 cloves garlic, crushed

1 jalapeño pepper, sliced

5-6 oz lite silken tofu

1/3 cup water

1/3 cup freshly squeezed lime juice

2 Tbs cider vinegar

2 Tbs chopped cilantro

1 tsp agave nectar

1/2 tsp cumin

1/2 tsp sea salt

Instructions (makes 2 cups)

IN A DRY HEAVY-BOTTOMED nonstick skillet on medium-high heat, add pumpkin seeds and tamari, mix well, and toast for 3-5 minutes, stirring constantly, until pumpkin seeds are golden and aromatic. Transfer them to the food processor.

In the same skillet, heat the oil on medium and roll it around the skillet. Add garlic and pepper, coat them in the oil, and sauté until garlic is fragrant. Add them to the processor with the pumpkin seeds.

Pulse the processor three or four times.

Add silken tofu, water, lime juice, vinegar, cilantro, agave nectar, cumin, and salt.

Process until smooth. If still warm, cool to room temperature or chill in fridge.

PEPITA VEGGIE DIP: Leave out the water and reduce lime juice to 1/4 cup.

Tangy Sour Cream

I almost exclusively want sour cream as a topper for Mexican dishes—chili, taco salad, and nachos especially—so I came up with this tangy sour cream which has flavors perfectly matched to Mexican dishes.

Ingredients

Instructions (makes about 2 cups)

1 12 oz package of lite silken tofu

1 tsp olive oil

3 Tbs lime juice (juice of one large lime)

2 tsp apple cider vinegar

1 tsp sugar

1/2 tsp salt

PLACE ALL INGREDIENTS in a food processor or blender and process until very smooth. Lasts up to a week in the fridge.

Nacho Sauce

There is nothing ground-breaking about this nacho sauce. It's yet another variation on the nooch sauce you'll find in almost every vegan cookbook. But this is my favorite and it works well on your Mexican dishes.

Ingredients

Instructions (makes 2 cups or so)

1 3/4 cups water

4 or 5 slices from small can of pickled jalapeño slices

1 cup nutritional yeast flakes

2 Tbs cornstarch

1 Tbs lime juice

3/4-1 tsp salt

1/2 tsp onion powder

1/2 tsp garlic powder

1/2 tsp cumin

1/8 tsp turmeric

MIX EVERYTHING IN A food processor or blender until it's completely blended. Transfer to a saucepan and whisk regularly (15 seconds out of every minute) over medium-high heat until thickened. Add 1/2 cup of salsa if you want to use it as a dip.

Guacamole

This makes just enough guacamole for two to have at it with a bag of chips and stop eating before they're sick or have ruined their dinners. Double or triple the recipe if you're making some for your family. This recipe prompted a marriage proposal from one of my testers, which is how a cookbook author knows she's done something right.

Ingredients

Instructions (makes about 1 ½ cups)

2 ripe avocados

juice of one large lime

2 garlic cloves, minced

2 stalks of green onions, white & pale green parts only, sliced thin

1 or 1/2 cup roma tomato, seeded (see Tips & Techniques, pg. tips 184) and diced

2 Tbs cilantro leaves, chopped

salt and pepper to taste

1 Tbs Tangy Sour Cream (pg. 86, optional)

SLICE THE AVOCADOS in half, peel off skins and remove pits, and add flesh to a small bowl. Squeeze the lime juice directly onto the avocado and then use a fork to smoosh the avocado and lime until texture is slightly chunky. Add garlic, green onions, tomato, cilantro, salt and pepper, and mix well. Add sour cream and mix again. Add more lime juice if desired. Serve at room temperature.

Mango Salsa

This is excellent as a dip, a veggie burger topper, spooned on top of grilled tofu, or inside a taco.

Ingredients

2 fresh mangoes, peeled and diced

1/4 cup unsweetened crushed pineapple

1 red bell pepper, seeded and diced

1 jalapeño pepper, seeded and minced

1 clove garlic, minced

1/2 red onion, diced small

2 Tbs chopped fresh cilantro or parsley

2 Tbs fresh lime juice

1/2 tsp sea salt

1/8 tsp cayenne pepper

Instructions

COMBINE ALL INGREDIENTS in a bowl. Serve immediately or store in refrigerator to allow flavors to blend even more.

MANGO-AVOCADO SALSA: Add one ripe avocado, cubed, in place of pineapple.

Raw Corn Salsa

If you haven't had corn fresh from the cob, you're seriously missing out.
This is perfect for those summer months when you can get corn super cheap at the
farmers market.

Ingredients

2-3 medium ears of uncooked corn,
cut from cob

2 medium tomatoes, finely diced

1 red bell pepper, finely diced

1 garlic clove, minced

2 stalks green onion, finely chopped

1 tsp olive oil

2 tsp fresh lime juice

2 Tbs cilantro or parsley, leaves
only, finely chopped

1/2 tsp sea salt

1/8 tsp cayenne

freshly ground black pepper to taste

Instructions (makes 4 cups)

MIX ALL INGREDIENTS in large bowl. Remove 1-2 cups of salsa; place in blender or food processor and blend well. Fold blended mixture back in with rest of salsa. Serve immediately.

GRILLED CORN SALSA: Before cutting the kernels from the cob, cut a lime in half and rub the halves directly onto the cobs of husked corn, then place the cobs directly onto the grill, and rotate regularly with tongs until corn is universally lightly blackened on all sides.

Birthday Salsa

This makes a lot of salsa. Usually the first thing that I do after making a batch of it is to jar a cup or two of it and give it to friends or keep it in the fridge to take to parties or send it in the mail to my friend Stefan for his birthday (hence the name).

Ingredients

Instructions (makes a ton)

1 red onion, roughly chopped

4 garlic cloves

1 poblano pepper, seeded and chopped

1 jalapeño pepper

1/4 cup lime juice

1 Tbs vinegar

1 Tbs flax oil or grapeseed oil

1 tsp paprika

2 tsp salt

1/4 cup cilantro leaves, packed

3 medium or 4 roma tomatoes, diced

PUT ONION, GARLIC, peppers, and lime juice in food processor and pulse 4 times. Add vinegar and oil and pulse a few more times. Add paprika, salt, cilantro, and 2/3 of your tomatoes, and pulse until it looks like salsa. Transfer salsa to large bowl and mix in the rest of the tomatoes by hand, mixing well. Chill in refrigerator for 1-2 hours before using.

Chipotle Ranch
Sandwich Spread

What do deli-style sandwiches have that yours are lacking at home? Most likely they use a secret sauce instead of regular old condiments, and it squelches around sandwich fixings, adds creamy goodness to every bite, and makes you weak in your knees. This is my secret sauce, and it beautifully complements your standard vegan sandwich fare: TLTs, roasted veggie sandwiches, veggie burgers, avocado and tofu sandwiches, pretty much anything. Just don't forget to at least lightly toast your bread or roll, as secret sauce will turn untoasted bread into a soggy mess in minutes.

Ingredients

Instructions (enough for 8-10 sandwiches)

1/2 cup silken tofu

1/4 cup vegan mayonnaise

1 chipotle pepper in adobo sauce, chopped

2 Tbs fresh parsley

1/2 tsp agave nectar

1/2 tsp onion powder

1/2 tsp garlic powder

1/2 tsp salt

1/4 tsp dill

1/4 tsp oregano

1/4 tsp thyme

pinch freshly ground black pepper

COMBINE ALL INGREDIENTS in a food processor or blender until smooth. Store in an airtight container in the fridge.

CHIPOTLE RANCH DIPPING SAUCE: Blend in 1/4 cup soymilk at the end.

Tapenade

I love tapenade as a sandwich spread for roasted and grilled veggies.

Ingredients

Instructions (enough for 4 sandwiches)

10 pitted kalamata olives, rinsed

10 pitted spanish olives, rinsed

1 Tbs capers, drained and rinsed

3 Tbs fresh parsley

2 garlic cloves

1 tsp lemon juice

1 tsp olive oil

tiny pinch salt

pinch freshly ground black pepper

ADD ALL INGREDIENTS to the food processor and pulse until chunky, scraping the bowl down about halfway through. Stores in the refrigerator for a couple of weeks.

Sunflower Feta

I use this tofu mixture whenever feta is called for. I love it as a salad or pizza topping.

Ingredients

14 oz firm tofu, drained

juice from one large lemon

1 Tbs white wine vinegar

1 tsp tamari or soy sauce

1 tsp grapeseed oil

1/2 cup raw sunflower seeds

salt

Instructions (makes 2 cups)

SQUEEZE EXCESS WATER from the block of tofu with your fingers and then crumble tofu into a medium size bowl with your hands until it resembles feta. Add lemon juice, vinegar, tamari, and oil and mix in well, with your hands or a spatula. Cover and place in refrigerator for 2-3 hours.

Remove tofu mixture from fridge and bring to room temperature. Using a blender or food processor, process seeds until crumbly. Add to tofu mixture and mix well. Add salt to taste and mix in well. Use immediately or return to fridge.

Vegan Parmesan

There is always a container of this parm substitute in my refrigerator. I wouldn't eat pasta without it. It mixes up in seconds and is much cheaper than the packaged variety available in stores.

Ingredients

1/2 cup walnuts

1/2 cup raw cashews

1/2 cup brown rice flour

1/2 cup nutritional yeast

1 Tbs garlic powder

2 tsp salt

Instructions (makes 2 cups)

COMBINE ALL INGREDIENTS in food processor and process until fine crumbs. Will last up to a month in an airtight container in your fridge.

Sides

Simply Sweet Potatoes

This is how I make sweet potatoes when I'm cooking a Southern meal. They're simple and sweet and complement Southern dishes like collard greens and black eyed peas perfectly.

Ingredients

Instructions (serves 4-6)

4 orange-fleshed yams, about 2 lbs.

2 Tbs non-hydrogenated margarine

2 Tbs tamari

1 Tbs maple syrup

1/8 tsp cinnamon

1/8 tsp ground ginger

1/8 tsp ground pepper

pinch of salt

PREHEAT OVEN TO 425°. Spray 9x13" baking dish with nonstick cooking spray.

Peel yams. Cut into 1" cubes and transfer to a large bowl.

In a small saucepot, heat margarine on medium-low until it melts. Add tamari, maple syrup, and spices. Whisk until combined.

Drizzle heated mixture on top of the yams. Use a wooden spoon or your hands to coat the yams well.

Transfer to the baking dish and arrange in a single layer.

Roast for 20 minutes. Remove from oven and move the potatoes around with a wooden spoon to keep them from sticking to the bottom of the pan. Roast for another twenty minutes. Allow to cool for at least 5 minutes before serving.

Braised Cauliflower

This is a basic way to braise cauliflower that infuses flavor into this vegetable that takes a lot of crap for being boring!

Ingredients

Instructions (serves 4)

2 tsp non-hydrogenated margarine

1 large head of cauliflower, cut into florets

pinch each of salt and pepper

1 cup vegetable stock

HEAT MARGARINE TO medium-high in stockpot or large shallow lidded skillet. Reduce heat to medium and add cauliflower florets.

Sauté, stirring if necessary, until each floret is is mostly golden brown on the surface. Add salt and pepper and vegetable stock and cover. Cook covered until cauliflower is tender and easily pierced with fork. Drain very well and serve immediately, maybe with some Lemon Tahini Dressing (pg. 84) drizzled on top.

Lemon Pepper Chard

I like to use rainbow chard in this recipe because of the pretty colors, but any chard will do.

I thought I'd mention here that I usually make a batch of this and put it in the fridge and heat it up the next day. I think it tastes even better when it marinates for a bit. But it's good either way!

Ingredients

Instructions (serves 4)

2 large bunches of swiss chard, de-stemmed and torn into pieces

2 Tbs red wine vinegar

1 Tbs balsamic vinegar

1 Tbs olive oil

3 cloves garlic

juice from one lemon

1/2 tsp freshly ground black pepper

pinch salt

STEAM CHARD UNTIL leaves are just wilted. Add rest of ingredients to a blender or food processor and pulse until well mixed. Toss chard with dressing in medium bowl, drain off the extra dressing, and serve immediately.

Collard Greens

Impress all your Southern friends by making greens that are flavorful without having been cooked with a giant hamhock for half the day.

Ingredients | Instructions (serves 2)

one bunch or 12-16 leaves collard greens

1 1/2 cups veggie broth

1/2 cup or one small red onion, chopped

4-5 garlic cloves, minced

1 tsp liquid smoke

1/2-3/4 tsp red pepper flakes

1/2 tsp salt

HEAT VEGGIE BROTH in a pot on medium heat. Separate the greens from their ribs. Chop them and add them to the pot. Add rest of ingredients. When broth reaches a boil, reduce to medium-low, cover, and cook until greens are soft, 2.5-3 hours. Check every 30 minutes and give it a good stir. When ready, drain (if necessary) and serve immediately.

Sesame Green Beans

I made a doubled recipe of this for my boyfriend's entire extended family the first time that I met them and for the rest of the trip, various members kept asking for the recipe, and when I gave it to them verbally, they'd ask, "That's IT?!" afterwards. That's it. I usually only use the almonds when I'm cooking for guests, since it adds a lot of fat to the recipe. But, you know, the good kind.

Ingredients

Instructions (serves 4)

1 Tbs sesame seeds

1/4 tsp salt

1 lb green beans, rinsed, ends snapped off and then snapped in half

1 tsp sesame oil, preferably toasted

2-3 garlic cloves, minced

2 tsp tamari or soy sauce

1/8-1/4 tsp freshly ground black pepper

1/8 tsp cayenne pepper (optional)

1/2 cup slivered almonds (optional)

TOAST SESAME SEEDS on a cookie sheet at 450° for 5 minutes or until they start popping. Remove from oven and set aside.

In large skillet or wok, bring 1 cup of salted water to a boil. Add green beans and blanch for 2-3 minutes, tossing regularly. Drain them and rinse with very cold water to stop the cooking process, then transfer them back to skillet or wok. Reduce heat to medium and add oil, garlic, tamari and pepper and toss well, coating the beans. Sauté for 8-12 minutes, continuing to toss regularly, until green beans blacken a little. Remove from heat and toss with sesame seeds and almonds, and another generous pinch of salt. Serve immediately.

Pickled Onions

These bright pink onions strips are delicious in tacos and burritos, or in green salads with vinaigrette dressing.

Ingredients

Instructions

2 large red onions

1/2 cup fresh lime juice

1/2 cup apple cider vinegar

1 tsp sugar

1/2 tsp salt

4 garlic cloves, crushed and then halved

1 Tbs black peppercorns

QUARTER THE ONIONS and then cut into very thin half-moons. Add onions to a heat-safe bowl and cover with boiling water. Set aside until tender, 2-5 minutes, and then drain. Leave onions in the colander while, in the bowl, whisk together lime juice, vinegar, sugar, and salt. Add garlic and peppercorns. Add onions back to bowl, cover with plastic wrap, and refrigerate for at least 4 hours, overnight for best results. Drain and serve at room temperature.

Creamy Herbed Polenta

If you're worried about your starch intake, polenta might be your new best friend. It rivals your favorite starches for amount of flavor and comfort food mouth feel, but with much fewer calories and carbohydrates.

In lieu of mashed potatoes, I love this creamy polenta as a bed for grilled veggies or tofu dishes. Likewise, you can allow the polenta to cool in tins or molds, refrigerate it, and slice it to replace pasta in dishes like lasagna.

Ingredients

4 cups water

1 tsp salt

1 cup polenta meal

3 Tbs soymilk or soy creamer

1 Tbs non-hydrogenated margarine

2 Tbs fresh basil, chiffonaded and then chopped

1-2 Tbs fresh parsley, chopped fine

1 Tbs fresh rosemary, dill, or thyme (according to taste) or 1 tsp dried

pinch freshly ground black pepper

Instructions (makes 4-6 servings)

BRING WATER WITH salt to a gentle boil in a large pot. Slowly add polenta, whisking continuously. Reduce to medium heat and cook, continuing to whisk, for 2-3 minutes. Cover, reduce heat to low, and simmer for 45 minutes, uncovering every 10 minutes to stir for a full minute and covering again. Turn off the heat and stir in soymilk, margarine, herbs, and pepper.

Serve warm, grits-style, or pour into a lightly sprayed muffin tin and allow to congeal to make individual polenta cakes.

PESTO POLENTA: Omit herbs and pepper and replace with 3 Tbs pesto.

Spiced Applesauce

Ingredients

Instructions (makes 4 cups)

3 lbs peeled, cored, and quartered cooking apples

1 cup water

juice of one medium lemon

1/2 cup dark brown sugar

2 tsp Chinese Five Spice powder

1/2 tsp salt

1/8 tsp ground ginger

ADD ALL INGREDIENTS to a large pot. Make sure lemon is clean and seeds are removed and add juiced lemon to the pot. Cover and bring to a boil. Lower heat and simmer for 20-30 minutes and remove from heat. Fish out lemons. Mash with potato masher. Allow to cool and store in an airtight container in the refrigerator.

Photo: Joni Newman

Lemon Rice

This tangy rice is a perfect complement to any tofu and potatoes meal. I hate to use the clichéd phrase "deceptively simple," but there you have it.

Ingredients

2 cups vegetable broth

1 cup uncooked long grain brown rice

1/2 tsp salt

1 Tbs non-hydrogenated margarine

zest and juice from one medium lemon

salt and freshly ground black pepper

Instructions (serves 4)

ADD BROTH, RICE, and salt to a lidded pot. Bring to a boil, reduce to a simmer, cover, and cook without stirring for 40-50 minutes or until broth is full absorbed.

Remove from heat. Fluff the rice with a fork. Add to the pot: margarine, lemon zest, and lemon juice. Season with salt and pepper to taste and serve immediately.

Green-wa

This is my all-time favorite way to make quinoa, which is why there are so many variations. The incredible smell that fills your kitchen when you make the green sauce will be enough to convince you to make this over and over.

Ingredients

Instructions (serves 4-6)

1 1/4 cup quinoa

2 cups water

2 tsp olive oil

2-3 garlic cloves

4 green onions

1/2 tsp curry powder

pinch of salt

3 loosely packed cups of spinach, washed well and torn

1/4 cup cilantro

1/4 cup plain soy yogurt

2 cups of frozen peas

RINSE QUINOA IN a sieve very well under cold water for 1-2 minutes to remove bitter coating from grain.

Add rinsed quinoa, water, and a pinch of salt to a pot and bring the mixture to a boil. Cover, reduce heat, and simmer for 15-20 minutes or until quinoa has totally absorbed the water. Unlike rice, it's okay to give quinoa a good stir when you check on it. When quinoa is fully cooked, take off the heat.

Meanwhile, slice green onions very thin and divide them into two piles: the white and pale green onion part and the bright green scallions. Set the scallions aside.

Heat oil to medium heat in a skillet. Add garlic and sauté for 1-2 minutes or until fragrant. Mix in onion part of green onions and sauté for another few minutes or until onion is bright green and tender. Add curry powder and mix well. Finally, add spinach to skillet, but don't mix in. When spinach is wilted (2-3 minutes), mix well with garlic and onion mixture and sauté for another few minutes.

Take mixture off heat and add to food processor or blender with cilantro. Blend very well. Scrape down sides, add soy yogurt, and blend again.

Steam frozen peas until tender. Combine cooked quinoa, cooked peas, and blended green mixture. Stir in scallions. Serve at room temperature. Add more salt at table if needed.

- -

MEGA GREEN-WA: Replace 1 cup of peas with 1 cup of green garbanzo beans. Add 1 cup of cooked green beans.

INDIAN GREEN-WA: Double the amount of curry powder and sub lite coconut milk for the soy yogurt. Top with 1/4 cup chopped unsalted cashews.

Photo: Jen Oaks

Roasted Garlic Mashed Potatoes

This "just for 2" recipe is how I make mashed potatoes when I'm cooking for just my boyfriend and myself. Double if you're cooking for a family.

Ingredients

6-8 garlic cloves, still in skin

3-4 yukon gold potatoes, mostly peeled, quartered

1/2 cup plain soy yogurt

1/3 cup soy or rice milk

salt and freshly ground black pepper to taste

Instructions (serves 2)

PREHEAT YOUR OVEN to 400°. Wrap garlic cloves in foil and toss in the oven for 30-40 minutes. Remove and allow to cool for 10 minutes or so before unwrapping.

Meanwhile, add peeled and quartered potatoes to a large pot. Add just enough cold water to cover the potatoes and salt liberally. Bring water to boil, reduce heat, cover, and allow to simmer for 20-30 minutes or until potatoes can easily be pierced through the center with a knife.

Turn off heat, drain, and return drained potatoes to same pot. Use potato masher to break down the potatoes. Add roasted garlic by squooshing the garlic right out of the skin like you'd push ketchup out of a packet and mash it into the potatoes. Add yogurt and soymilk and continue to mash until you reach your desired consistency. Add salt and pepper to taste.

GREEN ONION VARIATION: Stir in 3 stalks of thinly sliced green onions at the end and garnish with 2 Tbs minced fresh parsley leaves.

CARAMELIZED ONION VARIATION: Slice one shallot or half an onion into slivers and then sauté in olive oil until caramelized and stir into the potatoes at the end.

Stuffed Twice-Baked Potatoes

We sometimes will eat two halves of these potatoes as a main course, but they're best as a side in a comfort food meal.

Ingredients

Instructions (serves 3-6)

3 russet potatoes, cleaned well and halved

2 tsp olive oil

4 cloves garlic, minced

1/4 tsp crushed red pepper flakes

1/4 cup shallots, sliced very thin

1 bunch of broccoli, florets only, chopped

4 oz or about 1 cup mushrooms, sliced thin

1/2 tsp oregano

1/2 tsp thyme, dill, or rosemary

1 tsp tamari or soy sauce

salt to taste

PREHEAT OVEN to 400°. Place potatoes cut side down on a baking sheet and bake for 45 minutes.

Heat olive oil in large skillet to medium heat and add garlic, pepper, and shallots. Sauté until shallots are translucent. Add broccoli, mushrooms, and herbs to skillet along with 1/2 cup of water and tamari. Stir well and then cover, reduce heat to low, and allow to simmer for 10-15 minutes.

Scoop out baked potatoes, leaving a 1/4" inch or so layer of potato along the skins for stability. Add the potato directly to the skillet with the other vegetables and sprinkle with a little salt. Using a wooden spoon or a fork, mix the potatoes well with the stuffing. If you're making these for kids, you might want to add a tablespoon or so of non-hydrogenated margarine into the mix now. Add stuffing back into the potatoes and pop them back into the oven for another 15-20 minutes. Serve immediately, salting more at the table if necessary.

Roasted Roots

The greatest part about this recipe? If you don't like one of the root vegetables, just swap it out or use more of another that you do like. You can do all yams and carrots for an extremely orange side dish at Halloween or Thanksgiving. If you're a beet-hater, use more parsnips or add kohlrabi. Whatever you like.

Ingredients

3 medium carrots

1 garnet yam

2 medium yukon gold potatoes

1 parsnip

1 beet

1-2 Tbs olive oil

2 Tbs tamari or soy sauce

1/2 tsp maple syrup

1-2 garlic cloves

1 tsp thyme

1/2 tsp rosemary, crushed

1/2 tsp dill

1/2 tsp salt

1/8 tsp freshly ground black pepper

salt and pepper to taste

Instructions (serves 4-6)

PREHEAT OVEN to 400°. Peel all the roots and then chop them into 3/4-1" square pieces or so. In a large bowl, whisk together the resk of the ingredients. Add the roots and use your hands to toss them very well. If you use beets, the parsnips will turn a pleasing pink! So will your hands! Yay!

Add them to a lightly sprayed 9x13" baking dish. Roast for 20 minutes, remove from oven, toss roots around with a wooden spoon or spatula, put back in the oven and roast for another 20-30. Remove and serve immediately, although I tend to like it even better the next day and the next. Salt and pepper more at the table if needed.

Refried Black Beans

Use this recipe as a side for Mexican meals, a filling for burritos, or a topper on nachos.

I use primarily vegan mozz when I want to add a little cheesiness to my Mexican dishes because it's closest in flavor to queso blanco and queso fresco, the mild white cheeses used in Mexican cuisine. Yellow cheese and nacho cheese flavors are Tex-Mex-y and tend to be too strong and overshadow the flavors in your dishes.

Ingredients

1 15 oz can black beans, mostly drained or 1 1/2 cups cooked black beans with 1 Tbs of cooking liquid

1/2 cup red onion, diced

3-4 cloves garlic, minced

1 tsp cumin

1/4 tsp salt

1/8 tsp cayenne

1/4-1/3 cup veggie broth or water

1/4 cup grated and then crumbled vegan mozzarella (optional)

Instructions (makes 4 servings)

SPRAY A LARGE skillet with olive oil spray and bring to medium heat. Sauté onion and garlic for 5-10 minutes, stirring frequently, until onions are tender. Mix in cumin, salt, and cayenne and continue to sauté for another minute or so. Add black beans straight from can with a little bit of the liquid from the can, a tablespoon or so. Mix well. Add broth and mix again, covering and allowing to simmer for 8-10 minutes. Uncover, stir again, and remove from heat. Allow to cool for a few minutes and then, using a potato masher, mash beans very well directly in the skillet.

If you really like your refried beans whipped and creamy, you can blend them in the food processor or blender.

Transfer to a medium bowl and sprinkle vegan cheese on top.

Dirrrty Rice and Beans

This is a Cajun-Mexican fusion dish. Like most thrifty vegetarians, I've had about enough regular ol' rice and beans to last a lifetime. My rice and beans have to have kick now, and this recipe definitely kicks me in the pants.

The fake meat, by the way, is what's making your recipe dirrrty instead of just regular Mexican rice, so don't leave it out. If you want this to have a more Mexican flavor, choose soyrizo. If more Cajun, choose veggie sausage.

Ingredients

1/2 cup dried pinto beans

1/2 cup dried red kidney beans

1 cup long grain brown rice

2 cups veggie broth or water

2 bay leaves

salt

1/2 large red onion (about 3/4 cup), diced

4 oz soyrizo or vegetarian sausage

1/2 tsp cumin

1/8 tsp cayenne

1 chipotle pepper packed in adobo, minced

1/4 cup tomato sauce

1/4 cup chopped cilantro (optional)

Instructions (makes 4 cups)

SOAK DRIED BEANS in 2 cups of water for 8-24 hours. Drain.

Take out two pots. Fill one with a quart of water, add the beans and bay leaves and a liberal amount of salt, bring to a boil, reduce to simmer, and cover. Fill the other with 2 cups of broth and the rice, bring to a boil, reduce to simmer, and cover. Set timer to 30 minutes.

Check on rice when timer goes off—will likely need a good stir and another 10 minutes or so. Your beans aren't nearly done, so don't bother checking.

In the meantime, steam-fry your onion in a large non-stick, preferably cast iron skillet, over medium heat. When the onion starts to look a little soft and pinkish, scoot it over to one side of the pan and crumble your soyrizo or veggie sausage into the other side of the pan. Soyrizo will brown faster, so keep your eye on it and make sure to move it around.

Check your rice again. It's probably done. If it is, give it a good stir and take it off the heat. Check the beans while you're at it: take out one pinto and one kidney and let them cool down and then roll them between your fingers. If you still can't tell if they're done, pop one in your mouth. They probably need a bit longer. If they're done, drain them but don't rinse.

When fauxmeat is browned, integrate it with the onions. Sauté for another few minutes. Mix in cumin, cayenne, and chipotle pepper and about 1/2 teaspoon of salt. Add tomato sauce and cilantro, mix well, reduce heat to lowest setting. Keep this warm until beans are done.

When everything is ready, combine rice, drained beans (don't forget to remove the bay leaves), and meat mixture. You're done! Add a tablespoon or so of cilantro as garnish just before serving.

Main Dishes

Simple Chicken-Style Seitan

If you have tried making seitan before and it was a giant disaster or it took so much time that you swore you'd never bother again, try just this one last time and I promise that it won't disappoint.

The greatest thing about seitan is that, because of its texture, it works a million times better than tofu or tempeh as a meat replacement for both the homestyle casseroles from your childhood and the fancy wine-based sauces in your gourmet cookbooks.

Ingredients

broth:

6 cups cold veggie broth or 6 cups cold water and 1 vegetarian bouillon cube

1/3 cup soy sauce

1/2 cup chopped onions or 1 Tbs onion powder

2 bay leaves

2 Tbs dried sage

2 tsp thyme

1 tsp oregano

1 tsp rosemary

1 tsp savory (optional)

dry ingredients:

1 1/2 cups vital wheat gluten

1/3 cup chickpea flour (besan)

1/4 cup nutritional yeast

1 tsp onion powder

Instructions (makes 10-12 steaks or 14-16 cutlets)

MIX BROTH INGREDIENTS in a large pot on the stove. Make sure that all the liquids are cold—if you need to use a bouillon cube instead of veggie broth, just add the cube to the cold water, undissolved.

Mix dry ingredients in a large bowl. Mix wet ingredients in a small bowl. Add wet to dry and mix well. Knead the dough a little inside of the bowl to make sure all the dry ingredients are absorbed, then transfer to a clean surface and knead for a minute or two longer.

After you've worked with it for a few minutes, divide the mixture into even pieces. If you want steaks, you should make the pieces about 1 1/2" in diameter, the size of a cooked matzo ball. If you want cutlets, make it slightly smaller, about a rounded tablespoon. Then use your hands to make each piece as flat as possible. You should feel as if the dough is a little "springy" and massaging it with your fingers as you shape the pieces will make it look more meatlike when it's cooked.

1 tsp garlic powder

freshly ground black pepper

wet ingredients:

1 cup cold water

1 Tbs ketchup

2 Tbs tamari or soy sauce

After you flatten a piece, slip it into the broth. When all the pieces have been added to the broth, turn the heat on high. I don't care about the old adage: watch this pot until it comes to gentle boil and then immediately turn it down to a low simmer, cover it, and leave it for an hour.

Return, turn off the heat. Either use the seitan immediately or transfer it to a container for storage. Always store seitan in the cooking broth. Use a sieve to transfer the broth from the pot without any of the bay leaves or herbs—just straight broth. When the seitan is gone, you can use this broth instead of water to make rice, to boil potatoes, or pretty much anywhere veggie broth is called for.

Mustard Crusted Seitan

Mustard lovers! This one's for you.

If you've never tried panko, use this recipe as your excuse and I bet from then on, whenever the word "breadcrumbs" appears in a recipe, you'll see "panko."

Ingredients

4-6 Simple Chicken-Style Seitan (pg. 128) cutlets, still in their broth

2 Tbs brown mustard seeds

1/3 cup Dijon mustard

1 cup panko (Japanese bread crumbs)

2 Tbs chives, minced

1/2 tsp salt

1/4 tsp freshly ground black pepper

olive oil

Instructions (serves 3-6)

IF YOUR CUTLETS are more than 1/2" thick, consider cutting them in half. This recipe works best with thinner cutlets.

In a large dry skillet set on medium-high heat, brown the mustard seeds for a few minutes, tossing gently, until seeds begin to pop. Turn off the heat.

In one shallow bowl, add mustard. In another large shallow bowl or a plate, combine panko, toasted mustard seeds, chives, salt and pepper.

Coat the bottom of a large skillet with a thin layer of olive oil (2-3 t) and bring it to medium-high heat. When oil is heated through, lower to medium.

If you haven't already, remove the amount of seitan cutlets that you want to use and transfer them to a clean plate. It's okay if they are still a little drippy.

Set up a frying station next to your stovetop with the seitan plate, the mustard bowl, the panko mixture bowl and a plate with paper towels or paper bags to drain.

Using one hand (your "wet" hand), transfer a cutlet of seitan to the mustard bowl and spread cutlet with a very thin layer of the mustard. If you have a brush, you might want to try brushing the mustard on. Using the same hand, drop the coated cutlet into the breadcrumbs.

Now, using your other hand (the "dry" hand), flip the cutlet a couple of times in the breadcrumb mixture until it's lightly covered. Tap the cutlet to get rid of the extra. Immediately transfer coated seitan cutlet to the skillet.

Lightly fry each side for 5-7 minutes or until golden brown. Using tongs or a spatula, transfer cutlet to paper towels to drain. If you have to do these in batches and you're worried about the first batch getting cold, keep them warm in your oven once you've drained. Or just zap the first batch in the microwave for 30 seconds.

Serve with steamed asparagus, broccoli, or green beans.

Crispy Beer-Battered Seitan

Did you really expect me to put out a cookbook with no fried chicken recipe? Y'all, please.

For those of you who shy away from fried foods (and I am one of you), this one isn't so bad, especially since seitan is naturally fat free. But if you're really concerned, save it for a special occasion or make it for your veggie friend who has a yen for comfort foods.

Ingredients

6 steaks or 10 cutlets of Simple Chicken-Style Seitan (pg. 128) in broth

1/4 cup canola oil

1-1/2 cups panko or crushed cornflakes

1 1/2-2 cups unbleached all-purpose flour

1/4 cup nutritional yeast

1 Tbs garlic powder

1 Tbs assorted dried herbs of your choice (any combination of thyme, dill, rosemary, and oregano)

2 tsp onion powder

1 tsp salt

1/2 tsp paprika

1/4-1/2 tsp freshly ground black pepper

1 12 oz bottle amber beer

Instructions (serves 4-6)

PUT A DOUBLE layer of paper towels or paper bags on a large platter or cookie sheet and set aside on the back burners of the stove. On another large plate or shallow bowl, add panko and shake to distribute into an even layer and set aside.

In a heavy-bottomed skillet set to medium-high heat, add oil. Meanwhile, in a large mixing bowl, whisk together flour, nutritional yeast, garlic powder, herbs, onion powder, salt, paprika, and black pepper. Whisk in beer. Place on the boiler next to skillet (making sure boiler isn't lit, of course).

In batches: with one hand (your "wet" hand), immerse seitan piece in beer batter and flip around to coat well. Transfer immediately to skillet, the oil of which should be crackling and smoking a little—if it's smoking too much, turn down heat a tad. Allow to fry for 30-45 seconds and then flip over with tongs or a spatula and fry other side. Transfer immediately to the towel-lined platter to drain. Keep heat under skillet and again, turn down a little if it's smoking.

When all seitan pieces have been fried once and have cooled a bit, stack 'em on far side of platter and then double line the rest with paper towels. Set up a station: seitan pieces furthest from skillet, beer batter next, panko plate next, then skillet. Repeat frying process from above, except this time dip the seitan in panko after coating in beer batter and before frying. After both sides have fried to a golden brown, transfer them to drain again.

Serve immediately with gravy and steamed veggies on the side.

Tofu Marsala

This is a shameless attempt to recreate the Tofu Marsala from The Farm, a Portland restaurant. It is a bit more labor-intensive than most of my recipes, so I usually save it for a special occasion.

Ingredients

14 oz of firm tofu, drained and pressed very well for 2-3 hours

marinade:

1 cup Marsala wine

1/4 cup soy sauce

1 Tbs olive oil

3 cloves of garlic, pressed or minced

marsala:

1 Tbs olive oil

1 1/2 Tbs non-hydrogenated margarine

2-3 cloves garlic, minced

1/4-1/3 cup shallots or onion, diced

8 oz mushrooms, sliced

1/2 cup Marsala wine

1/2 cup vegetable broth

2 Tbs fresh parsley, minced

1/2 tsp oregano

1/2 tsp thyme

1/2 cup vegetable broth mixed with 1 Tbs cornstarch

1-2 tsp fresh lemon juice

salt and pepper to taste

Instructions (serves 4)

SLICE PRESSED TOFU lengthwise into 1/2" patties, and then in half again (a regular block of tofu would make 6-8 pieces). Whisk marinade ingredients and then soak tofu slices in marinade in the refrigerator, covered, for 4-8 hours ahead of time. If need be, rotate the slices from top to bottom so all slices get equal marinade. At time of cooking, slices should have uniform medium brown color.

Preheat oven to 200° and spray a cookie sheet with canola oil spray.

Remove your tofu from the marinade and pat dry.

Heat olive oil in a large skillet to medium-high. Reduce to medium and swirl pan to coat whole pan with thin layer of oil. Add tofu slices to hot oil. When brown and crispy, flip the pieces gingerly with tongs or spatula. Sauté other side in same manner and then transfer to paper towels to drain off excess grease. Finally, transfer the slices to cookie sheet and place in oven to keep warm.

If there is still any oil left in pan, compensate and add less margarine than is called for. Add margarine to skillet and when it's melted, add garlic and sauté for a minute. Add shallots and continue to sauté. When shallots are tender, add the mushrooms. Remove from the heat and add the Marsala. Return to heat and continue to sauté until Marsala is almost completely gone. Add the vegetable broth and herbs. Bring to a quick boil and then reduce heat to a simmer. Slowly add the stock mixed with cornstarch and mix in. Turn off the heat and add lemon juice, and a pinch each salt and pepper. Serve sauce over tofu slices with mashed potatoes or steamed veggies. Add more salt at the table if necessary.

Baked Mac and Cheese

I love homestyle mac and cheese, but can't get down with the all nutritional yeast sauces, or the recipes that have half a cup of oil or margarine. This is my compromise: creamy, rich macaroni and crusty goodness, with much less fat.

Ingredients

Instructions (makes 4-6 servings)

8 oz whole grain macaroni or elbow pasta

3 tsp non-hydrogenated margarine

4 tsp unbleached all purpose flour

1 1/4 cups rice milk

2 Tbs nutritional yeast

1/4 tsp salt

pinch nutmeg

pinch freshly ground black pepper

4 oz vegan cheddar cheese, shredded

1 slice of whole grain bread

2 tsp non-hydrogenated margarine

PREPARE MACARONI according to directions on package until noodles are al dente and drain. Spray an 8x8" baking dish with non-stick cooking spray.

Meanwhile, melt margarine in a medium, nonstick saucepan over medium heat. Add flour one teaspoon at a time and whisk until there are no lumps. Reduce heat to low and briskly whisk for one minute.

Slowly whisk in rice milk and bring to a simmer. Reduce heat to medium-low and simmer for 10 minutes, whisking for 10 seconds out of every minute as sauce thickens.

Whisk in nutritional yeast, salt, nutmeg, and pepper. Add vegan cheese and continue to cook until cheese melts, 6-10 minutes, whisking regularly.

Drain noodles if you haven't already, then return them to the pot in which they were cooked. Add cheesy sauce and stir well until pasta is coated. Pour into baking dish.

Toast bread and then pulse with margarine in a food processor or blender until they form fine bread crumbs. Sprinkle evenly over the top of the macaroni.

Bake at 350° for 25-30 minutes. Allow to cool for 5 minutes before serving.

Spinach Lasagna

This is my boyfriend's favorite meal. If he had his way, I would make this every single day.

If you can't find tomato basil marinara and you're too rushed to make my recipe, add 1/2 cup of fresh basil, cut in chiffonade (see Glossary, pg. 185) to your jar of sauce.

Ingredients

Instructions (serves 8)

tofu ricotta:

14 oz firm tofu, drained and very well pressed

2 Tbs lemon juice, or juice from half a large lemon

1/4 cup minced fresh parsley

1 tsp garlic powder

1/2 tsp sea salt

1/8 tsp freshly ground black pepper

lasagna:

8 wholegrain lasagna noodles

4 cups torn spinach or 8-10 oz baby spinach leaves

one recipe Marinara (pg. 76), blended smooth in a food processor or blender or 26 oz jar of tomato basil marinara

5 oz vegan mozzarella, shredded

2 Tbs vegan parmesan (pg. 100) (optional)

PREHEAT THE OVEN to 425°. Prepare the tofu ricotta and set aside.

Bring 2 quarts of salted water to a boil and cook lasagna noodles according to the direction on the package. Drain noodles but do not rinse them.

Blanch the spinach until just wilted, only a minute or so. Set aside.

Spray a 9x13" dish with olive oil spray. Ladle a thin layer of the marinara on the bottom of the dish. Arrange four of the lasagna noodles on top. Evenly distribute half of the tofu ricotta on top of the noodles. Then do a layer using all of the spinach. Drizzle about a 1/2 cup of the marinara on the spinach.

Add the second layer of noodles and distribute the rest of the tofu ricotta over the noodles. Pour the rest of the marinara on top. Top with shredded mozzarella and vegan parmesan.

Cover with foil and bake for 30-40 minutes. If after 40 minutes, the cheese isn't totally melted, move a rack of your oven to the top level and broil it uncovered for 2-3 minutes.

Butternut Squash Lasagna

If fall had a taste, it would be this lasagna. This is a great dish to make at Thanksgiving or for a friend who's just had a baby.

At first glance, this appears to be pretty labor intensive, but if you want to roast the squash and make the Béchamel Sauce the day before, you can knock out the rest of the prep work of this lasagna in a half hour, easy. Or make the whole thing on the weekend and eat it throughout the next week.

Ingredients

3 lb butternut squash

1 lb firm tofu, drained

12 whole grain lasagna noodles

1 Tbs olive oil

1 medium yellow onion, diced

2 cloves garlic, minced

2 Tbs fresh sage, chopped

1/8 tsp nutmeg

salt and pepper

1 recipe Béchamel sauce (pg. 78)

1 cup shredded vegan mozzarella (optional)

2 Tbs vegan parmesan (pg. 100, optional)

Instructions (serves 8-12)

PREHEAT THE OVEN to 450°. Cut each butternut squash in half lengthwise and scoop out and discard the seeds. Score a criss-cross pattern across the flesh of the squash and place cut side up, in a large roasting pan. Drizzle or brush with thin layer of olive oil. Cook on the top rack for 40 minutes until tender. Allow to cool for 10-20 minutes.

In a large bowl, crumble and squoosh tofu with your hands until it resembles ricotta and set aside.

In a large, heavy-bottomed skillet, heat 1 tablespoon of olive oil on medium heat. Add onion and garlic and sauté until onion is tender, 6-8 minutes. Scoop cooked squash from skins and transfer to skillet. Add sage, nutmeg, and pinch each of salt and pepper. Sauté for 4-6 minutes and then remove from heat.

Preheat oven again to 375°. Cook lasagna noodles according to directions on package and drain, but don't rinse.

In a food processor or heavy-duty blender, blend squash and onion mixture until smooth. Transfer all but a cup of it to the bowl with the tofu and mix gently—this is your filling.

Add béchamel sauce to remaining cup of squash mixture still in processor or blender and blend until smooth—this is your sauce.

Ladle small amount of sauce onto bottom of 9x13" pan. Arrange 4 lasagna noodles on top. Distribute half the filling in an even layer. Do another layer of noodles. Add the rest of the filling and then another layer of noodles. Pour the remainder of the sauce over the top.

If using vegan mozzarella and parmesan cheese, distribute in a thin layer on top of the sauce. Cover with aluminum foil and bake for 40 minutes.

Penne Alfredo

Ingredients

Instructions (serves 4-6)

3 cups whole grain penne pasta

2 Tbs non-hydrogenated margarine

1/4 cup raw cashews, minced

4 garlic cloves, minced

2 Tbs unbleached all purpose flour

1 1/2 cups soymilk

1/2 cup fresh parsley, minced

1 Tbs chopped fresh rosemary or
dill or 1 tsp dried

1/2 tsp Cajun spice (pg. 158,
optional)

freshly ground black pepper and
salt to taste

PREPARE PASTA ACCORDING to instructions on packaging.

Meanwhile, in a small saucepan, heat margarine on medium until melted. Make sure that cashews and garlic are minced very fine and add to saucepan. Heat until garlic is fragrant, stirring regularly, about 2 minutes.

Add flour 1 tablespoon at a time to garlic and cashew mixture, making a roux. Add soymilk slowly, a half cup at a time, whisking thoroughly. Continue to cook over medium heat for 5 minutes, whisking every minute or so. Turn off the heat and stir in parsley and spices. Add immediately to cooked pasta and serve.

Photo: Shayne Berry

Pasta E Fagioli

Pasta Fazool! Pasta E Fagioli literally translates as "Pasta and Beans." In Italy, it's a soup served as a meal, since Italian soups are extremely hearty and essentially just a bowl of food swimming in delicious broth. Have I mentioned that I love the Italians?

Ingredients

Instructions (makes 6 servings)

2 tsp olive oil

3/4 cup or one medium onion, diced

3-4 garlic cloves, minced

2 ribs celery, halved and diced

1 28 oz can diced tomatoes, with juices

1/2 cup packed fresh parsley, chopped

1/2 tsp oregano

1/2 tsp thyme

1/2 tsp crushed red pepper flakes

1/4 tsp dried basil

2 cups veggie broth

1/2 cup dry white wine

1/2 lb whole grain tube pasta

2 cups spinach

15 oz can white northern beans, drained

1 tsp salt

1/4 tsp freshly ground black pepper

1 tsp sugar

vegan parmesan (pg. 100) for garnish

IN A LARGE SKILLET, heat olive oil to medium heat. Add onion, garlic, and celery and sauté until vegetables are soft, stirring frequently, 4-6 minutes. Add tomatoes, parsley, oregano, thyme, crushed red pepper, and basil and mix in well. Sauté for 2-3 minutes or until it begins a soft boil. Add veggie broth and white wine. Reduce to low and cover.

In a large pot, bring 2 quarts of water to a boil. Add pasta. Boil for five minutes max. Drain.

Transfer contents of skillet to still warm pot and reduce heat to medium. Add drained pasta to pot. Cover and cook for 15 minutes.

Add spinach, beans, salt, pepper, and sugar to pot. Cover again and cook for another 5 minutes.

Serve immediately in a bowl and garnish with vegan parmesan and parsley leaves.

Kasha Varnishkes

This is one of the favorite recipes of my Jewish boyfriend from his childhood. If you time it well, you can make this on three burners of your stove all at once and have dinner inside of 20 minutes.

Everyone who's tested this wants me to tell you upfront that it tastes better reheated the next day, but I wouldn't know because my boyfriend and I can't make this last until the next day. We can't. We eat the first serving and then another a few hours later and then the next thing you know, it's gone. So you'll just have to take their word for it.

Ingredients | Instructions (serves 2-4)

2 1/4 cups water

1 cup whole buckwheat groats (kasha)

salt

1/4 tsp ground cumin

1 Tbs olive oil

1 large yellow onions, quartered and then thinly sliced

2 garlic cloves, minced

2 cups whole wheat farfalle (bowtie) pasta

freshly ground black pepper to taste

BRING THE WATER to a boil in a pot over high heat. Stir in kasha, a pinch of salt, cumin and 1 teaspoon of the olive oil, reduce the heat to low immediately, cover, and cook for 12-18 minutes, or until water is fully absorbed. Remove from heat and set aside.

Heat remaining 2 teaspoons of olive oil in a skillet on medium. Add the onions and garlic and a pinch of salt and sauté, stirring occasionally, for 6-8 minutes. Reduce the heat to low, and cook for 10-12 more minutes, stirring occasionally, until onions begin to caramelize.

Meanwhile, bring 2 quarts of water to a boil in a large pot. Add a few pinches of salt. Add the pasta and cook according to the directions on the package. Drain the pasta and toss the pasta with the onions. Fluff the kasha with a fork and then combine with pasta and onions. Season with salt and pepper to taste.

Serve as is or with a doubled recipe of Mushroom Gravy (pg. 82).

Grilled Portobellos

If you're like me, shelling out for portobellos feels like such a splurge, so I like to treat my shrooms right by giving them a good wine marinade bath before grilling.

Don't be afraid of cleaning your mushrooms well. Alton Brown proved in an episode of Good Eats that, contrary to popular belief, mushrooms hardly absorb any water during a rinse, and since these caps are immediately plunged into a marinade, it won't affect the texture at all.

Ingredients

1 cup dry white wine

1 cup veggie broth

1/2 cup olive oil

juice from two large lemons

3 Tbs balsamic vinegar

4-6 garlic cloves, crushed and then chopped

1/4 cup shallots, chopped

1/2 cup fresh parsley, chopped, or half parsley/half basil

1/2 tsp kosher or sea salt

1/4 tsp freshly ground black pepper

4 large portabello mushrooms, destemmed, cleaned, and patted dry

Instructions (serves 2-4)

IN A LARGE, SHALLOW, lidded airtight container, briskly whisk together wine, broth, olive oil, lemon juice, and vinegar. Add garlic, shallots, parsley, salt, and pepper and mix in. Submerge portabello caps in the marinade. Don't worry if there's not enough surface area of the container for all four caps to be submerged in the marinade—it's okay if one or two are resting on top. Place in refrigerator for 24 hours, rotating caps about halfway through.

Whether you're using an outdoor grill or a grill pan on the stove, bring the heated surface to a medium-high heat. Mushroom caps should sizzle and smoke while they're grilling—there is no need to add additional oil to the surface because the shroom has sucked up enough marinade.

Grill both sides of the mushroom for 2-3 minutes each. Mushrooms will shrink to 3/4-4/5 their pre-cooked size while grilling.

Serve immediately on their own, as you would your favorite veggie burger, or slice for on top of a salad.

Asparagus with Spinach and Artichoke Cream Sauce

If you can't find white asparagus, just use all green asparagus.

Ingredients

Instructions (makes 4-6 servings)

1 lb white asparagus

1 lb green asparagus

sauce:

1 Tbs non-hydrogenated margarine

2 garlic cloves, minced

2 cups soymilk or 1 cup soymilk and 1 cup soy creamer

4 Tbs nutritional yeast

1 tsp garlic powder

1/2 tsp dill

1/2 tsp thyme

1/2 tsp salt

1/4 tsp freshly ground black pepper

1 Tbs all purpose flour

6-8 oz spinach, well cleaned and torn into small pieces or baby spinach leaves

1/2 can of artichoke hearts, drained and quartered

CUT THE WOODY parts off the end of the asparagus stalks. Peel lower two thirds of each stalk with a vegetable peeler. Cut stalks into 2-3 in pieces and then rinse. Cook white and green asparagus separately in 2-3 quarts of boiling salted water, uncovered, until just tender, about 5 minutes for white, a little less for green. Drain well in a colander and rinse under cold water to stop the cooking process, until asparagus is cool. Drain and pat dry with paper towels.

In a small saucepan, heat margarine over medium heat until melted. Add garlic and sauté until browned and fragrant. Add soymilk, nutritional yeast, garlic powder, herbs, salt, and pepper. Whisk until smooth and cook, 3-4 minutes, whisking once a minute or so. Add flour slowly, about one teaspoon at a time, and whisk until it dissolves before adding more. When all the flour is added, lower the heat to medium-low and cook for 5-7 minutes.

In another pot, blanch the spinach. Transfer to sauce and stir in. Separate leaves of the artichoke hearts and stir in.

Serve sauce over the asparagus on a bed of creamy herbed polenta, brown rice, or roasted garlic mashed potatoes.

KALE AND MUSHROOM CREAM SAUCE: Replace spinach with kale and replace artichokes with 4 oz of sliced mushrooms that have been sautéed in 1 tsp margarine.

Thai Bowl

Do I need to explain that this is about as far from authentic Thai cooking as I am physically from Thailand right now? I didn't think so.

Ingredients

4 oz uncooked rice noodles

2 cups mung bean sprouts

1 head broccoli

1 carrot

1 cucumber

1/2 cup cilantro, chopped

1/2 cup peanuts, chopped

lime wedges for garnish

sauce:

3 Tbs fresh lime juice, or juice from one medium lime

2 Tbs peanut butter

2 Tbs rice vinegar

2 Tbs water

1 Tbs soy sauce

1 Tbs peanut oil

1 Tbs mirin

1 Tbs brown sugar

1 Tbs fresh mint leaves, diced

1 1" square peeled piece of ginger, minced

1/8 tsp chili oil or hot sauce

Instructions (makes 4 servings)

SEPARATE THE BROCCOLI crowns from the stems and then cut the crowns into small pieces. Lightly steam then set aside.

Peel the carrot and grate, with food processor or by hand. Peel the cucumber in stripes, then halve the cucumber. Use a spoon to de-seed the cucumber, then grate the cucumber with food processor or by hand. Put broccoli, carrots, cucumbers, bean sprouts, and cilantro in a large bowl and set aside.

Combine all ingredients for the sauce in a blender and process until smooth.

Meanwhile, boil the rice noodles according to the directions on the package.

At this point, decide if you want to serve the noodle bowl hot or cold.

If you're serving it hot, drain the noodles when they're fully cooked and transfer them back to the pot. Pour the sauce over the noodles, bring the heat to medium-low, and stir until noodles are well coated. Remove from the heat and transfer them to the bowl with the veggies and toss with the veggies until well-mixed. Garnish with crushed peanuts and lime wedges and serve immediately.

If you're serving it cold, drain the noodles and rinse with cold water until the noodles are chilled. Add the noodles to the veggies and toss well. Pour the cold sauce over the entire bowl and toss to coat again. Garnish with peanuts and lime wedges and serve.

Sloppy Joannas

Hey baby, I wouldn't put my name on something unless I were really proud of it, and this is hands down the best sloppy sandwich I've put in my maw. It's even picky kid approved!

You can control the sloppy factor of this recipe by deciding how much tomato sauce to add. I like mine kind of dry and usually only use 8 oz, but if you prefer the cafeteria-style, sauce-on-your-face, mega-sloppiness, bump it up to 15 oz. Some of my testers also chose to add chopped green bell peppers, a vegetable that I am pretty sure is the incarnation of pure evil, but if you don't mind concentrated evil in your food, go right ahead.

Ingredients

1 cup TVP

7/8 cup veggie broth or vegetarian "beef" broth

1/2 cup or 1 small yellow onion, diced

3 garlic cloves, crushed and then chopped

1 Tbs brown sugar

8-15 oz canned tomato sauce, preferably no salt added

1 tsp cumin

1 tsp yellow mustard

1/4 tsp liquid smoke

1/4-1/2 tsp salt

¼ tsp freshly ground black pepper

1/8 tsp cayenne (optional)

4 whole grain buns

Instructions (makes 4 sandwiches)

HEAT BROTH OVER medium heat in a saucepan and add TVP. Stir and cook until TVP has absorbed broth, 2-5 minutes.

Spray a large skillet with olive oil cooking spray and heat to medium. Add onion and sauté for 5-6 minutes, stirring frequently with a wooden spoon. Add garlic and sauté for another 5-6 minutes or until onion is tender and browning and garlic is fragrant. Sprinkle brown sugar over onion and garlic and mix in well with spoon. Continue to sauté for another 8-10 minutes, stirring regularly, until onion is really soft and caramelized.

Add tomato sauce, cumin, mustard, and liquid smoke and mix well. At this point, you might want to transfer the sauce to a food processor or blender, blend it, and then transfer the sauce back to the pan, especially if you're making these for children who squawk at the sight of vegetables. Add TVP and mix well. Add salt, black pepper, and cayenne and mix well again. (Use less salt if tomato sauce had salt in it.)

Reduce heat, cover, and allow to simmer for 15 minutes, uncovering and giving it a good stir every 5 minutes.

Toast buns open-faced in oven or toaster oven. Spoon good sloppy amount onto each bun and serve immediately. Garnish with tomato slices, lettuce, and pickles if so desired, but expect to be regarded with derision by sloppy joe purists. Devour. Start cooking the next batch while the sauce is still in the corners of your mouth.

Chana Masala

When I put the first draft of this recipe up on my website, I called it "White Girl Chana Masala," because I make no claims to authenticity. I just wanted to make an at-home version of one of my favorite Indian restaurant meals. This was the result after a few attempts and fine-tunings.

Ingredients

Instructions (makes 6 servings)

2 cups veggie broth or water

3 cups cooked chickpeas or 2 15 oz cans chickpeas, drained

2 tsp peanut oil

1 tsp brown mustard seeds

1 tsp cumin seeds

2 cups diced onion

2 garlic cloves, minced

2 Tbs ginger, minced

1 cup diced tomatoes

1/4 tsp turmeric

1/4 tsp cayenne

1 tsp garam masala

the juice of one lime

cilantro and mint leaves for garnish

PUT ONE CUP of the chickpeas and one cup of the broth into the food processor and blend. Set aside.

In a skillet, heat peanut oil over medium-high heat. Add the mustard and cumin seeds and sauté, stirring, until they pop. Lower to medium heat and add the onions, garlic, and ginger, and sauté until soft. Add the tomatoes and cook for an additional 5 minutes or so. Now add the chickpeas, the blended chickpeas, turmeric, cayenne, and garam masala. Stir well. Add a cup of broth, bring to a boil, reduce the heat, partially cover the skillet with the lid (an overturned cookie sheet works), and cook for 30-45 minutes, stirring every 10 minutes or so.

Remove from the heat and stir in the lime juice. Garnish with chopped cilantro and whole mint leaves. Serve with brown basmati rice.

Cajun Spiced Tofu

I love this tofu sliced on top of pasta dishes to "kick it up a notch." Get it? BAM!
Get it? Shut up, that's an awesome joke.

You can use commercial Cajun spice in this recipe if you have it, but it's been my
experience that it's usually way too salty, so I like to make my own. Use the leftovers
as an excuse to try veganizing some of your favorite Cajun dishes.

Ingredients

Cajun spice:

2 Tbs paprika

2 Tbs garlic powder

1 Tbs freshly ground black pepper

1 Tbs onion powder

1 Tbs oregano

1 Tbs dried thyme

2 tsp cayenne pepper

2 tsp salt

*Add all ingredients to a jar or
plastic lidded container, add lid,
shake well.*

Main ingredients:

14 oz firm tofu, drained and well-
pressed

1 cup soymilk

1 Tbs cornstarch

2 Tbs cajun spice

1 cup cornmeal

Instructions (serves 2-4)

MOVE THE TOP rack of your oven to the very highest level
and set the oven on broil. Spray a cookie sheet with olive
oil spray.

Cut tofu into 4-5 1/4" thick slabs. Whisk soymilk, cornstarch, and 1 tablespoon of the Cajun spice in shallow
bowl until cornstarch dissolves.

Combine cornmeal and remaining tablespoon Cajun
spice on a plate.

Dredge each piece of tofu in soymilk and then cover in
cornmeal mixture, shaking off excess. Arrange breaded
tofu on the cookie sheet in a single layer, and then do a
light coating of spray on top.

Put the cookie sheet in and closely monitor the progress
so it doesn't burn. (Most people leave the oven cracked
open while broiling.) Check every 15-30 seconds and
pull it out when it starts to brown. Flip the tofu and broil
the other side.

Allow to cool for 5-10 minutes before cutting into strips
and serving.

Photo: Shayne Berry

White Beans and Kale

Dear working stiffs! I made this one just for you. Do the simple prep in the morning before you leave for work. Come home, kiss your pretty partner, put the beans on the stove, make a cocktail, watch the Daily Show, and then prepare the rest of the meal in less than 10 minutes. You're welcome!

Ingredients

1 cup of dried white beans

1 large or 2 medium heads of kale (4-6 cups)

1 medium lemon

1 bay leaf or 1" piece of kombu

1 1/2 tsp olive oil

1 large shallot or half a large yellow onion, sliced into slivers

3 garlic cloves, sliced into thin slivers

3/4-1 tsp of salt

1/4-1/2 tsp freshly ground black pepper

Instructions (serves 4)

IN THE MORNING: Rinse the beans and then soak them in 2-3 cups of water. Set aside. De-stem the kale leaves, rinse them well and pat (or spin) dry, and transfer them to a very large bowl. Squeeze the juice from a lemon onto the kale and then, using your hands, massage the lemon juice into the kale while tearing the kale into smaller pieces. Leave the bowl on the counter.

When you get home: Add 4 cups of water and bay leaf to a large saucepot, salt liberally, and bring the water to a boil. Meanwhile, drain the beans and rinse them. When water is boiling, add the beans, reduce the heat to medium-low and cover. Go do something else for a half hour or so.

Come back and take a bean out to taste it. It will probably still be al dente. That's fine—they probably need another 10 minutes or so. If they're soft already, drain them immediately.

Meanwhile, add 1/2 teaspoon of the oil to your largest skillet and heat it to medium-high. When oil is hot, reduce to medium and add shallots and garlic to the pan. Coat them well in the oil and sauté for 5 minutes or so. Add all of the kale—it might not seem like it will fit but

160

kale wilts extremely quickly. Add salt and pepper and another 1/2 teaspoon of oil and sauté for 5-10 minutes, stirring frequently if not constantly. Turn heat to low.

Check the beans again. They should be ready by now. Drain them and add them to the skillet. Mix well and add the final 1/2 teaspoon of oil to pan. Serve immediately, on its own or over brown rice or multigrain pasta. Take those leftovers to work tomorrow.

Black Bean and Sweet Potato Flautas

Black beans and sweet potatoes: the new peanut butter and jelly. I called it first!

If you want, you can completely cheat with these and use canned refried black beans and mashed canned sweet potatoes, and the total prep and cook time would be under a half hour. Leftover flauta filling, if there is any, tastes great heated up with brown rice the next day.

Ingredients

2-3 sweet potatoes or yams, peeled

1 recipe Refried Black Beans (pg. 122) or 1 15 oz can low fat vegetarian refried black beans

2 tsp chili powder

1 cup frozen corn, thawed to room temperature

1 medium tomato, diced

juice from one lime

12 6" corn tortillas

Instructions (serves 4-6)

PREHEAT OVEN TO 425°. Wrap peeled sweet potatoes in foil and pop them in the oven for 40-60 minutes or until they are soft. Remove from oven, leaving oven on, and allow them to cool.

Meanwhile, in a medium-sized bowl, mix refried black beans, corn, and tomato with chili powder and lime juice.

Cut sweet potatoes into 2" chunks and then, using potato masher or fork, mash the sweet potatoes until they are chunky.

Spray a cooking sheet with olive oil spray. Assemble flautas by filling the first third of each tortilla with 2-3 tablespoons each of the sweet potatoes and black bean mixture. Roll tightly and hold closed with a toothpick. If the corn tortillas start to fall apart a little bit, don't worry, that's natural and they will still look and taste great. Arrange side by side on cooking sheet and then spray lightly with olive oil spray. Bake for 10 minutes.

Serve warm with guacamole and salsa.

Tamale Pie

Tamale pie recipes are part of our American heritage—they date back to at least 1911! Those recipes probably didn't contain seitan or soy cheese, but I'm sure that's only because it wasn't an option yet.

Ingredients

polenta crust:

1 cup cornmeal

2 1/2 cups veggie broth

1/2 tsp salt

sauce:

1 large onion, chopped

4 garlic cloves, minced

1 Tbs chili powder

1 tsp cumin

1 15 oz can diced tomatoes, drained

1 8 oz can of tomato sauce

fillings:

1 1/2 cups cooked or 1 15 oz pinto, kidney, or black beans, drained and rinsed

2 cups frozen corn, thawed and drained

2 cups browned Simple Chicken-Style Seitan (pg. 128) strips, taco meat from Taco Salad (pg. 58), or browned soy chicken strips

1/2 cup shredded vegan nacho cheese or 1/2 cup Nacho Sauce (pg. 88, optional)

Instructions (serves 8-12)

PREHEAT OVEN TO 400°. In a pan, steam-fry (see Glossary, pg. 185) the onions and garlic on medium-high heat. When soft, reduce to medium, add the spices, and sauté for another 5 minutes. Add the tomatoes and tomato sauce. Stir thoroughly and allow to simmer for 10-15 minutes and then take it off the heat.

Combine cornmeal, veggie broth, and salt in a pot and bring to a boil. Reduce to a simmer and stir constantly until thickened, about 5 minutes. Spray a 9x13" baking pan with oil spray and spread most of the polenta along the bottom in an even layer, leaving 3/4 cup of polenta leftover.

Add fillings to the casserole dish in layers. Wait until the sauce has been off the heat for 10 minutes or so and then pour it on top of all the fillings. If using, add shredded vegan cheese or nacho sauce on the top in an even layer. Add the rest of the polenta in dollops on the top. Cover the dish with a lid or aluminum foil and bake for 30 minutes.

Allow to cool for 5-10 minutes before cutting and serving. Garnish with avocado cubes, chopped cilantro, Tangy Sour Cream (pg. 86), or fresh salsa. Or nothing!

Better-than-Basic Veggie Chili

What makes this recipe better than your current standby "open a bunch of cans and throw everything in a pot" chili recipe? The key to this recipe is keeping half of the onion crisp and to not overcook the chili. When chili stays on the burner for hours and hours, it loses the individual flavors and turns into mush. With this recipe, total preparation time is minimal, which makes it perfect for a family or a weekday night. This freezes well and like all good chili, tastes even better the next day.

Ingredients

Instructions (serves 8)

1 14 oz can tomato sauce

1 large onion, diced

4 garlic cloves, minced

6 medium tomatoes, diced or 28 oz canned diced tomatoes, with juice

2 canned chipotle peppers or 1 large jalapeño pepper, minced

1 tsp cumin

2 bay leaves

1 1/2 cups cooked or 1 15 oz can pinto beans, drained and rinsed

1 1/2 cups cooked or 1 15 oz can black beans, drained and rinsed

1 1/2 cups frozen or fresh or 1 can corn, drained

salt to taste

IN SAUCEPOT OR crockpot, simmer the garlic and half of the chopped onion in tomato sauce for 10 minutes or so on medium-high until the onion is nearly translucent. Lower the heat and add the tomatoes, peppers, and cumin. Simmer, covered, for 10 minutes. Add the bay leaves and beans and simmer for another 30 minutes. Finally, add the corn and the rest of the onion and simmer for another 10 minutes. Turn off the heat, fish out the bay leaves, and serve immediately with your favorite garnishes.

Ingredients (continued)

any of the following for garnish:

cubed avocados

chopped cilantro

shredded vegan nacho cheese

rounds of green onion

dollop of Tangy Sour Cream (pg. 86)

Northwest Meets Southwest Chili

Do not be afraid of the brewed coffee in this chili! It adds depth and flavor and an almost smoky quality to the recipe.

Ingredients

Instructions (serves 6 to 8)

7/8 cup vegetarian "beef" broth or veggie broth

1 cup dry TVP

2-3 chile peppers

2 tsp olive oil

4 cloves garlic, minced

1 yellow onion, diced

6 medium tomatoes, diced or 28 oz canned diced tomatoes, with juice

1/2 cup brewed espresso or strong brewed coffee

1 1/2 cups cooked pinto beans or one 15 oz canned, drained and rinsed

1 1/2 cups cooked black beans or one 15 oz canned, drained and rinsed

1 1/2 cups cooked kidney beans or one 15 oz canned, drained and rinsed

1/8-1/4 tsp cayenne pepper

1 tsp cumin

1 tsp cocoa powder

salt to taste

BRING THE BEEF broth to a boil in a pot, add the dry TVP. Remove from heat when TVP has absorbed all the broth. Put TVP aside.

Preheat your oven to 450°. Place peppers on cookie sheet or pan and roast the peppers on the top rack of the oven for 5-7 minutes, rotating or turning them after 3. Take the peppers out of the oven and place them in a plastic sealable bag and let them sweat for 10-15 minutes. When they're done, peel the peppers, cut them open, and remove the majority of the seeds. Since the seed of the pepper determines their heat, you can leave some or most of the seeds if you want your chili really hot. I usually leave a few. Put on gloves and cut the peppers up fine or put them in the food processor to dice them.

Ingredients (continued)

any of the following for garnish:

cubed avocados

chopped cilantro

shredded vegan nacho cheese

rounds of green onion

dollop of Tangy Sour Cream (pg. 86)

Sauté onions and garlic in olive oil in a saucepot until onions are clear—add a little water to the pot if the onion starts to stick; mix in TVP. Sauté for an additional 3-5 minutes.

Use blender or food processor to blend half of the tomatoes. Add blended tomatoes and diced tomatoes to the pot, then the rest of the ingredients, including the diced peppers. If you've left some of the seeds in the peppers, you might want to skip the cayenne altogether, depending on how much of a heat freak you are.

Reduce heat and simmer for one hour, giving it a good stir with a wooden spoon every 15 minutes. Serve with your favorite garnishes, adding more salt to taste if necessary.

Sweet Things

Aloha Bread

This is my veganized and reduced fat version of my favorite banana bread from childhood, which I found in one of those "ladies of the church" cookbooks of which my mom had a dozen. I don't keep half of these ingredients stocked, so when I'm craving this bread, it is part of the ritual to go shopping for the orange, coconut, and pineapple.

Ingredients

1/2 cup mashed very ripe banana (about 1 large)

1/4 cup applesauce

3 Tbs soy yogurt

2 cups flour

3/4 tsp baking soda

1/2 tsp salt

1/2 tsp cinnamon

1/4 tsp nutmeg

1/2 cup sugar

2 Tbs canola oil

1 Tbs molasses

1 Tbs or so grated orange zest

1 Tbs juice from can of pineapple

1 tsp vanilla

1/2 tsp almond extract

1 cup flake or shredded coconut

1/3 cup canned crushed pineapple, drained

1/2 cup crushed walnuts (optional)

Instructions (makes 8-10 large slices)

PREHEAT OVEN TO 375°. Spray a bread tin with nonstick cooking spray, preferably with flour added.

In small bowl, mash banana, then combine with applesauce and yogurt. Set aside.

Sift the flour, baking soda, salt, cinnamon, and nutmeg in a medium bowl.

In a large bowl, mix the sugar, oil, and molasses using a wooden spoon. Add the mashed banana mixture, orange zest, and pineapple juice and mix again. Finally, mix in the vanilla and almond extracts.

Add dry ingredients to wet in batches, folding each batch into the wet mixture before adding the next batch. Be careful not to overmix.

Fold in coconut and pineapple.

Dump into bread tin, using spatula sprayed with nonstick cooking spray to even out the batter if necessary. Sprinkle walnuts on top if you're using them. Bake on the lower rack for 25 minutes, take out and rotate 180 degrees and put it on the top rack for 10-20 more min-utes. A toothpick inserted in the middle should come out almost completely clean—maybe a dry crumb or two.

Take out and invert onto a cooking rack and then flip upside down (easy with two cooling racks sandwiching the loaf). Let cool for four hours before serving. Store wrapped in aluminum foil. Freezes very well!

Cherry Compote

When it comes to cherry picking in the summer, my eyes are perpetually bigger than my stomach. I scurry up trees with a basket around my neck and pluck every beautiful Bing and Rainier cherry that I see, and then come home, realize my folly, and immediately start pulling out my pie and crumble recipes to use up all those cherries.

This compote is a unique and alternative solution to cherry overload, and a jar of compote makes a great hostess gift for a summer party.

Ingredients

1 lb cherries, pitted

1/3 cup water

1/3 cup orange juice

1/4 cup sugar

3 Tbs fresh lemon juice

zest from half a lemon

1 Tbs cornstarch

2 Tbs kirsch, Cointreau, or Triple Sec

Instructions (makes 4-6 servings)

IN A MEDIUM saucepan, combine the cherries, water, orange juice, sugar, lemon juice, and zest. Bring to a boil and then reduce the heat to medium and simmer for 15-20 minutes, stirring occasionally. In a small bowl, whisk the cornstarch with the liqueur until it dissolves and add to the cherry mixture. Return to a boil and cook for 1 minute, stirring.

Reduce the heat to medium-low and simmer until thickened, 4-6 minutes.

Serve warm over soy ice cream, cheesecake, pie, or stirred into your oatmeal in the morning. Store jarred or in an airtight container in the refrigerator.

Soft Oatmeal Cookies

I psychotically love oatmeal cookies, and this is exactly how I like them: very soft, not too sweet, and a little salty.

Feel free to add raisins, nuts, or chocolate chips to make them the oatmeal cookies of your dreams! I love them just how they are.

Ingredients

1/4 cup non-hydrogenated margarine, softened

3/4 cup brown sugar

1/4 cup sugar

1 Tbs molasses

1 tsp vanilla

1/2 cup silken tofu, blended

1 1/2 cups unbleached all purpose flour

1 1/4 cups oats

3/4 tsp salt

1/2 tsp baking soda

1/4 tsp cinnamon

Instructions (makes 30ish cookies)

PREHEAT OVEN TO 350°. Spray cookie sheet with nonstick cooking spray.

In a large bowl, mix together margarine, sugars, molasses, vanilla, and silken tofu. In a separate bowl, combine the flour, oats, salt, baking soda, and cinnamon. Combine the dry ingredients with the wet ingredients and mix until just combined.

Drop the dough with a tablespoon onto cooking sheet. Then, using a little dish filled with water, wet your fingers to gently flatten each cookie until they are uniform and about 2 inches in diamater. Bake for 8-10 minutes. They might seem underbaked, but they're not!

Allow to cool on the sheet for 5 minutes before transferring them to cooling racks. When completely cool, store them in airtight containers with a piece of bread to keep them soft.

OATMEAL CREAM PIES: Double the cookie recipe and shape cookies slightly larger and thinner: 2 1/2" diameter and 1/4" thick. Cream together: 2 tsp hot water, 1/4 tsp salt, 8 oz vegan marshmallow cream, 1/2 cup softened non-hydrogenated shortening, 1/3 cup powdered sugar, and 1/2 tsp vanilla extract. Spread a thin layer of cream on flat underside of one cookie, then sandwich with the flat underside of another cookie.

Gluten-Free Chocolate Chip Bars

Vegetarians, be kind to your friends with wheat allergies! They are just as sick of going to social events and having nothing to eat as we are. Shower your sympathetic affection upon them in the form of these rad chocolate chip bars.

Ingredients

2 cups brown rice flour

1/4 cup cornstarch

3 Tbs tapioca flour

1 tsp xantham gum

1 tsp salt

1 tsp baking soda

1/2 cup + 1 Tbs non-hydrogenated margarine, melted

1/4 cup applesauce

1 cup brown sugar

1/2 cup sugar

1/2 cup silken tofu, blended

2 tsp vanilla extract

1 1/2 cups nondairy chocolate chips (or small chunks)

Instructions (makes 18-24 bars)

PREHEAT OVEN TO 375°. Create an aluminum foil hammock (see Tips & Techniques, pg. 184) in a 9x13" baking pan and spray with nonstick baking spray, preferably with flour added.

In a medium bowl, sift together flour, cornstarch, tapioca flour, xantham gum, salt, and baking soda.

In a large bowl, whisk melted margarine, applesauce, and sugars together. Add blended tofu and vanilla and mix well.

Using a rubber or silicone spatula, fold the dry ingredients into the wet ingredients until just combined, being careful not to overmix. Fold in the chocolate chips and then dump entire mixture into your hammocked baking pan. Use your spatula to gently pat down the batter evenly into the pan.

Bake until bars are golden brown, 25-30 minutes. Halfway through baking, rotate the pan 180° in the oven.

Allow to cool in pan for 5-10 minutes (baking pan should be cool to the touch), then use the hammock to transfer the bars to a cooling rack and allow to cool all the way to room temperature before cutting.

Store bars in an airtight container with a slice or two of bread so that they stay moist, as gluten-free baked goods tend to get dry.

Mojito Pie

Feel free to replace some or all of the water in the pie filling with light rum for true Mojito flavor.

Ingredients

Instructions (makes 8-10 servings)

crust:

3 Tbs non-hydrogenated margarine, melted and cooled

1 1/2 cups vegan graham crackers

1/2 tsp salt

1/4 tsp cinnamon

filling:

1/2 cup fresh lime juice

1/2 cup water

3/4 cup sugar

1/4-1/3 cup mint leaves

12 oz silken extra firm tofu, drained of extra water

2-3 tsp lime zest

extra mint leaves for garnish

IN A SAUCE PAN—not cast iron—bring lime juice, water, sugar, and mint leaves to a gentle simmer over medium-high heat. Whisk well until sugar dissolves, reduce to medium-low heat, and cook for 20-40 minutes, giving it a good stir every 10 minutes or so, until sauce is considerably thickened and has reduced down to a light syrupy consistency. Take off the heat, fish out the mint leaves with a spoon, and allow to cool to room temperature.

Preheat oven to 375°. Spray a pie or tart tin with non-stick cooking spray.

In a food processor or blender, combine melted margarine, graham crackers, salt, and cinnamon and process until fine crumbs. Dump graham cracker combination in the pie tin and, using your fingers, press it down into an even crust.

In a food processor or blender, combine syrup with tofu and lime zest and process until completely smooth. If necessary, use a rubber spatula to scrape down the sides and process again.

Pour mixture into the pie tin. Bake for 35-45 minutes.

Remove from oven and allow to cool for a minimum of two hours. Pie will be way too unstable to cut or eat before it has cooled completely, so leave it alone. Serve at room temperature or chilled. Garnish with whole mint leaves.

Lemon Almond Cake

This is a wonderful cake for summer afternoons when strawberries are ripe and inexpensive.

Ingredients

Instructions (makes 8-12 slices)

1 cup whole wheat pastry flour

1/2 cup unbleached all purpose flour

1/2 tsp baking powder

1 tsp baking soda

1/4 tsp salt

1 cup sugar

1 1/2 tsp almond extract

1/4 cup canola oil

1 cup almond milk or soymilk

2 Tbs lemon juice

zest from half a lemon

1/2 cup slivered almonds

8-10 strawberries

glaze:

1 cup powdered sugar

3 Tbs non-hydrogenated margarine, melted

2 Tbs fresh lemon juice

PREHEAT OVEN TO 350°. Using nonstick cooking spray, grease an 8x8" baking dish and set aside.

In a large bowl, sift together flours, baking powder, baking soda, and salt. In a medium bowl, whisk together sugar, almond extract, oil, almond milk, lemon juice, and zest. Add wet ingredients to dry ingredients and mix well. Pour into baking dish and bake for 22-25 minutes. Do the toothpick test in the center to make sure it's done. Set it aside to cool for 10 minutes.

De-stem strawberries, then cut in four slices from stem to tip. Arrange strawberries and slivered almonds in attractive layers on top of cake. I like to cover the whole surface with strawberry slices and then make "flower petals" on top with the almonds.

In a small bowl, whisk together powdered sugar, melted margarine, and lemon juice, until well-combined and there are no lumps of powdered sugar. Drizzle evenly over entire cake. Serve at room temperature.

Spice Cake

Ingredients

1 cup whole wheat pastry flour

1/2 cup all purpose flour

1 tsp baking powder

1 tsp baking soda

1/2 tsp cinnamon

1/2 tsp ginger

1/2 tsp allspice

1/4 tsp ground cloves

1/2 tsp salt

1 cup brown sugar

1/4 cup spiced applesauce

2 Tbs oil

1 Tbs vinegar

1 tsp vanilla

1 cup cooled chai tea or water

cream cheese frosting:

4 oz vegan cream cheese, softened

1 Tbs non-hydrogenated margarine, softened

3/4 cup powdered sugar

Instructions

PREHEAT OVEN TO 350° and spray an 8x8" baking dish with nonstick cooking spray.

Sift together flours, baking powder, baking soda, spices, and salt in a large bowl. In a medium bowl, stir together sugar, applesauce, oil, vinegar, vanilla, and chai.

Combine dry and wet ingredients and mix well with a spoon until combined. Pour into dish and bake for 25 minutes or until toothpick comes out clean.

Meanwhile, mix together cream cheese, margarine, and powdered sugar.

When cake has cooled (20 minutes or so), spread cream cheese frosting evenly on cake and serve.

Tips & Techniques

ALUMINUM FOIL HAMMOCK: When baking bars or brownies, line your baking dish with an aluminum foil hammock so it's easier to get those edge and corner pieces out without crumbling or sticking. Line the baking pan with two sheets of foil placed perpendicular to each other, with at least four inches "extra" foil on each side. After removing dish from the oven, allow to cool until aluminum foil is cool to the touch, then use the foil "handles" to transfer to cooling racks.

BANANAS: Bananas can be stored in the refrigerator, with their skins on, for longer keeping. They won't ripen any further, but the banana will stay fresh. You can also peel them, cut them into pieces, and store them in a sandwich bag in the freezer to easily add them to smoothies. If bananas have over-ripened to perfect banana bread dark black squooshiness but you're not ready to use them yet, you can also peel them and freeze them for that purpose.

BEANS: When you make beans for a recipe, make a little extra and store the leftovers in the freezer in two cup portions for easy use.

BREADCRUMBS: Store the ends of your quality loaves of bread in the freezer. When you need breadcrumbs, take out one slice per 1/2 cup of breadcrumbs needed, toast it, and pulse it in the food processor or blender.

BROTH: If you live in an apartment and don't have a garden or compost heap, you can store the skins, peels, and ends from your veggies in a large plastic zippered bag in the freezer. When the bag is full, simmer contents of bag in a quart of salted water for a few hours, and then transfer to a storage container, using a sieve to strain out all the pieces so it's straight broth.

CITRUS JUICING: Nuking a citrus fruit in the microwave for 15 seconds and then rolling it on the counter before you cut it will get you more juice.

GINGER: When you buy ginger root, peel the entire root and put it through the grater on the food processor. Freeze half and put half in your fridge for easy use.

SEEDING TOMATOES: Seeded tomatoes add

tomato flavor to dishes without adding the fluid. Cut tomato in half from side to side rather than from top to bottom. Over a trashcan or plate, gently squeeze the tomato half to loosen the seeds, and use your fingers or a paring knife to remove the seeds and majority of the pulp, leaving just the walls of the tomato.

STORING LEFTOVER LIQUIDS: Use ice cube trays and muffin tins to make single uses of pesto, wine for wine sauces, veggie broth, tomato paste, and coconut milk. What you do is pour the liquid into the wells of the tray, pop it in the freezer, and 24 hours later, transfer the cubes to a freezer bag and wash the tray.

Glossary

AGAVE NECTAR (OR AGAVE SYRUP): A sweetener commercially produced in Mexico from several species of agave. Agave nectar is sweeter than honey, though less viscous.

BLANCH: To plunge food into boiling water briefly, then immediately into cold water to stop the cooking process.

CHIFFONADE: Technique by which herbs or leafy green vegetables (such as spinach and basil) are cut into long, thin strips by stacking leaves, rolling them tightly, then cutting across the rolled leaves with a sharp knife, producing fine ribbons.

CHOP: Cut food into bite-sized pieces without worrying about consistency of size or shape. A food processor can be used to quickly chop.

DICE: To cut food into small equal-sized cubes, about 1/4" x 1/4".

EMULSIFY: Combine two liquids which do not mix well, e.g. oil and water, usually by whisking or shaking.

FLAX SEEDS: High in Omega-3 fatty acids, flax seeds are a must-have for the vegetarian kitchen. When ground into flax meal and combined with water, they become very viscous, making them an excellent egg replacer in pancakes and muffins. Whisk one tablespoon flax seeds, ground, with three tablespoons water to equal one egg.

KNEAD: Kneading is done by hand with a pressing-folding-turning action performed by pressing down into the dough with the heels of both hands, then pushing away from the body. The dough is folded in half and given a quarter turn, and the process is repeated.

MINCE: To cut food into very small pieces, smaller than chopped.

MIRIN: A sweet rice wine similar to sake, but with a much lower alcohol content.

NUTRITIONAL YEAST: Not to be confused with brewer's yeast, nutritional yeast is a nutritional supplement that it is an excellent source of protein and vitamins. It has a nutty, cheesy, creamy flavor, which makes it popular as an ingredient in cheese substitutes.

POLENTA MEAL (OR POLENTA GRITS): Course ground cornmeal used for making polenta. Regular cornmeal can be used, but most natural foods stores sell a cornmeal in bulk that is specifically designed for polenta, labeled as "polenta meal" or "polenta grits," or even just "polenta."

SILKEN TOFU: Silken tofu, not interchangeable with soft tofu, comes in a variety of firmnesses and is used predominantly in this cookbook as a thickener and to add creaminess to a recipe without much added fat. There are two types of silken tofu currently commercially available: one is asceptically packaged and is on the shelf at the grocery store, sometimes with the Oriental foods, and the other type is stored in water and is in the refrigerated section with the rest of the varieties of tofu. I have specified when one is needed over another, but most of the times that silken tofu is called for in this book, either is fine.

SIMMER: To cook food in liquid at a temperature low enough that tiny bubbles just begin to break the surface.

STEAM-FRY: To cook food, usually vegetables, without any fat on a fairly high temperature, allowing the natural moisture in the food to release and cook the food.

SWEAT: A technique by which food, particularly vegetables, is cooked in a small amount of fat over low heat, so that the food softens without browning, and cooks in its own juices.

TVP: Texturized Vegetable Protein, also sometimes called Texturized Soy Protein (TSP), is a meat substitute made from defatted soy flour, a by-product of making soybean oil. Quick to cook, high in protein, and low in fat, TVP is extremely versatile, and so porous that it quickly absorbs the flavors of the liquids and seasonings in which it's cooked, with a mouth feel that is very similar to chopped meat.

VITAL WHEAT GLUTEN: Available in the bulk section of natural foods stores, vital wheat gluten is the natural protein found in wheat, is 75% protein, and is essential in making seitan.

Index

Dear beloved cookbook owners,

This is not a full index of every single ingredient in every recipe, just the key ones. Oils, broth, garlic, dried spices, salt and pepper—things like this were left out, because listing every recipe they are in would be tedious and pointless, don't you think? So please enjoy this almost complete index of the cookbook.

Love,
Joanna

Index

Index

Index

Index

Index

Index

Index

Index

Index

Index

Index

Index